War and Grace

Short biographies
from the World Wars

Don Stephens

Evangelical Press (EP Books), an imprint of 10Publishing
Unit C, Tomlinson Road, Leyland, PR25 2DY, England
www.epbooks.org
epbooks@10ofthose.com

First published August 2005
Reprinted 2014
This edition 2021

British Library Cataloguing in Publication Data available

ISBN: 978–0–85234–594–8

To my wife and daughter,
Hazel and Heather,
with love and thanks

Contents

Illustrations

Foreword

Once you start this book you will not want to put it down. It is a collection of remarkable stories told by a master storyteller. My friend Don Stephens of Liverpool is a modest man who writes to interesting people all over the world. He is also a meticulous historian and competent theologian. But I know him best as the man who can hold congregations of children, teenagers and adults spellbound as he tells them of people and events that they have never heard of. Until now his work has only appeared in magazines. How good it is to see a number of his unpublished stories brought together in a book!

What shall I say about the thirteen brief biographies that you have in your hand? They are all true, not only in their general outline, but also in their details. They deal with people and events connected with the two World Wars. Each one, in its own way, is both exciting and moving. They tell us about men and women from very varied backgrounds—British, American, Dutch, German and Japanese. So what did these people have in common? During the turbulent events of those momentous years, God was at work in their lives. He brought these thirteen people to trust, know, love and serve the Lord Jesus Christ, and therefore to give themselves to the service of others.

A book like this cannot leave you unaffected. If you are already a Christian it will strengthen your belief in the sovereignty of God and in the transforming power of his gospel. It will also challenge you about the depth and consistency of your commitment to Christ. If you are not yet a Christian this book will remind you that it is God himself who takes the initiative in every conversion,

that he never turns away anyone who wants him, and that he
supernaturally sustains us in our life of discipleship. Whoever you
are, you will certainly join with me in urging Don Stephens to
bring out another book of stories just as soon as he can.

Stuart Olyott
Pastoral Director of the Evangelical Movement of Wales

Preface

I t was my mother speaking: 'He went away one man, and came back different.' My young ears listened. The words were intended for the lady she was talking to. However, it wasn't hard to put two and two together. The man who 'came back different' was my father.

I hadn't known him before the Second World War, only afterwards. By all accounts, he was a zealous Christian so shocked by the massive slaughter in the First World War that he had become virtually a pacifist. Then, in May 1941, one of Hitler's aircraft on a raid over Liverpool dropped a bomb that flattened a house and killed a family he knew. Within a week, he volunteered to fight in the British army, believing it was his Christian duty to do so.

That decision had far-reaching consequences. He was badly injured in North Africa in the struggle against the Germans and Italians. Action in southern Italy followed. Then he was brought back to England to train for D-Day. From 'Gold' beach in Normandy, he fought across France, Belgium, Holland and into Germany until the final defeat of the Nazis.

Later, when asked if he regretted being a volunteer when technically over age, he said, 'No, I would go through it all again; we had to fight to stop Hitler.'

I started to read about the war. Fascinated by aircraft, I joined the Royal Observer Corps, and became an early member of Air Britain (The International Society of Aviation Historians). My first printed writings are in its publications. With some friends, I helped found what was to become the Merseyside Aviation Society. My university studies inevitably included history.

While working at a comprehensive school at Halewood, Merseyside, in the 1970s, I connected my Christian outlook with the interest in the wars, and searched for people whose true stories could be shortened for use in Religious Education lessons and assemblies. I felt then, and still do, that God's providence guided me to those people and to those stories that would be told in this school—and others in which I worked. The Bible came first as far as I was concerned; these stories illustrated its themes and teaching in ways people of our time would understand. In adapted forms, many have also been used very successfully in various church projects. Some parts have been used as sermon illustrations. Many times it has been reported that the Holy Spirit used these accounts to bring to readers who had no previous interest in spiritual things meaning in life and the joy of forgiveness.

The First World War (1914–1918) and the Second World War (1939–1945), and their consequences, inevitably dominate the history of the twentieth century. It might be thought that those not born until later would not be interested in such terrible events. Yet what do we find? Libraries have well-used sections on these wars. The TV schedules list programmes that endlessly explore often obscure aspects of those turbulent times, as well as producing major series about them. Books with First and Second World War themes pour from publishing houses, and most are republished quickly. Even the arts, notably poetry and music, express particular features of the times.

But one topic is usually overlooked. It is the activities of Christians in those grim years. Part of my research is presented in these chapters. The results are sobering, moving and challenging. Because this book is genuinely 'different', I hope that these biographies will not be routinely dismissed as 'just another book about the war'.

Obviously, not everybody is interested in the history of these titanic struggles. Yet very large numbers of people, both men and women, are fascinated by almost all the varying aspects of them, even though most experienced none of it personally.

My own motivations are no secret. My parents both became Christians in a Presbyterian church in the Everton area of Liverpool in the years between the wars. They were people of the Bible; so when I came to personal faith in Christ aged eighteen it is not surprising that, after thought and careful study, I became a Reformed Christian in the same theological tradition. Later, I worked with, and respected, Christian friends who differed from me in some matters of interpretation and in style of worship. However, they did not disagree with the basic Christian beliefs common to all who base their faith on the Bible. The essential thing I discovered was not a theology, but a life-changing relationship with God. That is what you will find in the lives dealt with in this book.

In a world where fear, war and terrorism are still causing human tragedies, these stories show how the grace of God will always triumph where evil seems to reign. It is my hope that these biographies will be used by God to speak to people of the twenty-first century.

In essence, my motive is the same as that of the Bible writer who said, 'These [things] are written that you ... may have life' (John 20:31).

Don Stephens

Acknowledgements

In writing this book I have incurred many debts of gratitude, and I am happy to take this opportunity to thank those who have helped in its preparation.

Instead of all the names of my friends and colleagues appearing in these pages in one long list, I direct readers to more appropriate locations.

The names of many of my friends and helpers are in the boxes headed 'More information about …' that appear at the end of each story. Some are mentioned in the text of the stories. Others are named in the references to books and magazines in the endnotes. I thank them all for support, permissions, contributions and other forms of assistance. Help came from many sources and in differing ways. In most cases I have offered thanks privately as well as in this public way.

In addition, I feel considerable gratitude to friends who gave me appraisals and ideas at the earliest stages of the writing of each story. In alphabetical order they are: Hilary Creed, Arthur Howe, George Jones, John Ransom and Jean Vann.

I am also very grateful to those who helped me with images. Their names are listed in the section following the endnotes headed 'Picture credits'.

Organizations and publishers are almost entirely acknowledged in the endnotes, though some are referred to in the boxes providing further information at the end of each chapter. I found that many members of staff were very helpful beyond the call of duty, and hope they see this note of thanks.

I express my sincere gratitude to Stuart Olyott for contributing the foreword.

Thanks also to Brian Williams, who repaired my computer when required; Malcolm Evans, who frequently 'adjusted' it; and K. Paul Austin, who searched the Internet for obscure details.

I am grateful to the staff of Evangelical Press, particularly Senior Editor Anne Williamson and General Manager Anthony Gosling, for their sound advice, skill and encouragement.

It is possible that I may have omitted somebody who should have been acknowledged. I hope that I may be graciously forgiven.

Don Stephens

1

Louis Zamperini

Trouble, torment and forgiveness

Zamperini, who was five feet nine inches tall, was reduced to a skeletal sixty-seven pounds. Six weeks earlier he could have run a mile in just over four minutes and weighed 165 pounds. On 13 July 1943 he could barely crawl out of the raft onto the Japanese patrol ship.

Louis Zamperini in 1945

1

Louis Zamperini[1]

- A juvenile delinquent in California.

- An Olympic runner at the Berlin Games of 1936.

- An Air Force bomb aimer, decorated for gallantry in action.

- A survivor of forty-seven days adrift on a life raft.

- An ill-treated prisoner of war of the Japanese for two and a half years.

- A drunkard who almost wrecked his marriage.

- A Christian.

All these statements relate to the extraordinary life of Louis Zamperini.

The story begins when Louis Zamperini's father, Anthony, left Italy to make a new life in America. Louise, his mother, though born in America, was half Italian and half Austrian. They were an honest, hard-working couple, the sort who wanted to pay cash for things or do without. Louis was born in New York in 1917. He had a brother, Pete, who was two years older, and two younger sisters, Virginia and Sylvia.

When Louis was two and Pete was four, they both contracted double pneumonia. After their recovery, the doctor advised a move to a warmer climate. California was mentioned. As a result of the doctor's advice, the family moved west. In 1920 Torrance became home. It was then a small industrial town on the outskirts of Los Angeles.

The everyday language used in the laughter-filled home was Italian. When Louis started school the laughter stopped. The other boys and girls picked on him because of his poor English and Italian accent. Jeering groups of cruel children would provoke him so that he would swear in Italian. Louis' anger and unhappiness exploded in bad behaviour. By the age of seven he was 'that tough little kid down the street'. There was a chip on his shoulder. He smoked, played rough and cursed freely.

In spite of a supportive background, his rebellion grew steadily worse. By the time he was twelve he had a gang of other social misfits to mix with. Stealing became a sport—everything from chocolate bars to car parts. One of his favourite tricks was to steal beer and whisky from bootleggers knowing that they dare not report him. It was the era of 'prohibition', when possession of alcohol was illegal in America. Anybody who crossed him was in danger. Once or twice he was in frenzied fights during which he lost control of himself, beating his enemy in a most bloodthirsty and dangerous way.

As each day passed he grew more touchy and defiant. His worried parents upset him when they asked, 'Why can't you be a good boy like your brother?' All he could say in reply was that they picked on him, and cared more for Pete. His mother itemized his faults and then broke down in tears.

Louis hated both police and school. The chief of police in Torrance took him round the cells to see men locked up, telling him, 'We are warning you; this is where you will end up if you don't change.'

One summer holiday he ran away for a time with a friend. They jumped onto a freight train and hid in a boxcar. There were drink-sodden tramps on this train going to San Diego. On the way home one of them fell onto the rails when the train lurched round a bend. The tramp was cut to pieces. The hideous sight had no effect on Louis.

Pete was fed up with police coming to the family home about his younger brother. Without Louis' knowledge, his mother and Pete discussed the problem with the school principal. The school had a scheme of punishments already lined up to control the troublesome teenager.

The principal listened to Pete's plan. If Louis were given a clean slate, Pete would try to interest his brother in sport, especially running. As a result, in February 1932, when Louis was fifteen, he started the new school year without having to face a backlog of punishments.

Eventually, Louis Zamperini started to be recognized for his sporting prowess. On one occasion he heard pupils from his school shout, 'Come on, Louie!' This startled him because he was convinced that nobody knew or cared about him. Gaining recognition on the running track began to change his attitude. The direction of his life altered. He started to train and get fit every day of the year, whatever the weather, and gave up smoking while in training. He also applied himself to his studies. Though Pete was a fine runner, he quickly recognized that Louis was better. He paced Louis and encouraged him.

Louis Zemperini in training at the Olynmpic Village, Berlin, in 1936

During the next three years Louis never lost a race. Local sports writers called him 'iron man' and 'leather lung'. At the age of nineteen, Louis was selected to be one of the 334 American athletes to go to the 1936 Berlin Olympic Games. City businessmen donated his suitcase. It had 'Torrance Tornado' stencilled on its side. The delinquent had come a long way in a short time.

The Berlin Olympics of 1936 presented Louis Zamperini with a range of new experiences. As the youngest man in his event, the 5,000 metres, he did well to be the first American to finish, although in eighth place. After the race he was disappointed, but remembered a conversation with Pete: 'You will have to be patient. You won't be in your prime until the 1940 Games.' Louis consoled himself with thoughts about the future. Pete was right. He would be twenty-three in 1940. His coach agreed with Pete. With more practice, strength and experience, Louis Zamperini could be a winner.

At the 1936 Games he shared a room with Jesse Owens, a black sprinter who won four gold medals. Hitler showed his racism by deliberately refusing to shake hands with Owens, but he did ask to see Zamperini. Louis had run an exceptional last lap in fifty-six seconds. Hitler congratulated him on his record-breaking effort. Later he was asked for his impressions of Hitler. His response was: 'Even if Hitler had given me his wristwatch it wouldn't have meant much. He was just another dictator. At the time I didn't understand politics, and was more concerned about other things than how the world worked—or didn't.'

Later, he and a friend spent a summer evening in Berlin city centre. They were souvenir hunting. 'I wanted a Nazi flag the most,' Louis remembered. Spotting a Nazi banner up a pole on the Reich Chancellery's perimeter wall, he climbed up and grabbed it. There were shouts and the sound of a gunshot. The guards brought General Werner von Fritsch to confront Zamperini and his friend. 'Why did you tear down the swastika?' the general wanted to know. When Zamperini replied, 'To remind me of the wonderful time I had in Germany,' he was given the banner!

The welcome home was tumultuous. At the formal reception, the police chief remarked, 'After I chased Louie up and down every back alley in Torrance, he had to be in shape for *something*.' The comment stuck in Zamperini's mind because it reminded him how close he had come to being permanently on the wrong side of the law.

In the autumn of 1936, he was admitted to the University of Southern California. In 1938 he ran a mile in 4.08 minutes and broke the National Collegiate record. Two years later he finished an indoor mile at Madison Square Gardens in New York in 4.07. He began to dream of being the first man to run a four-minute mile. In fact, it was more than a dream. Commentators on athletics considered it a real possibility. It was not to be.

The military clique that ruled Japan in the 1930s had illegally invaded Manchuria and China. As a result, the 1940 Tokyo Olympic Games were cancelled. Zamperini's dreams of athletic fame came crashing down.

On 29 September 1941 a new phase of Louis Zamperini's life began when he joined the US Army Air Force. Determined to become an officer, he studied hard at Officers' Candidate School. In August 1942 he graduated as second lieutenant. By then Pearl Harbor had been attacked and the United States was at war.

On 25 October 1942 his posting came through. He was assigned to Hawaii to join the 42nd Squadron of the 11th Bombardment Group. This unit flew B-24 Liberator bombers. Zamperini was the bombardier in the ten-man crew. The bomber he flew in had 'Superman' painted on the nose by the crew, with the familiar comic character holding a bomb pointing downwards.

What followed was anything but comical.

Zamperini's first raid was on Christmas Eve 1942. The squadron was to be the first to bomb Japanese-held Wake Island. 'Superman' was one of twenty-six Liberators on the mission. At the time Zamperini attributed their success to luck. People often called him 'Lucky Louie'. After the raid he jogged along the beach near Kahuku airfield. It was his way of keeping in trim. The post-war Olympics were always in his mind. Would his luck hold?

During numerous reconnaissance and search missions, 'Superman' survived when other B-24s were lost in various ways. Louis' legendary 'luck' stood with him.

In mid-April 1943 the twenty-six Liberators were flown to Funafuti (now called Tuvalu) in the Ellice Islands. From there they were ordered to bomb Nauru. This island held a huge deposit of phosphate, needed by the Japanese for fertilizer and explosives. 'Superman' and its crew of ten unloaded its bombs. From his position in the perspex nose, Zamperini counted nine Japanese Zero fighters take off. That caused anxiety because the Liberators had no friendly fighters protecting them.

Three Zeros peeled off to attack 'Superman'. Cannon shells and bullets smashed into the bomber. The radio operator, Sergeant Brooks, was hit in the chest. Zamperini gave him a shot of

A B-24 Liberator bomber, the type of aircraft in which Louis Zemperini flew on missions with the 42nd Squadron

morphine. While helping Brooks, Zamperini felt blood dripping down the back of his neck. He discovered that Sergeant Pillsbury, in the upper gun turret, had had his toes shot off. He too needed morphine. Zamperini now moved to the centre of the plane. Four men were lying there. The blood-spattered scene looked as if a bomb had exploded. Zamperini and the two pilots were the only men without serious injury. After this attack, and all the damage sustained by the bomber, 'Superman' was fortunate even to reach base and land safely.

While the seven men were rushed away for emergency surgery, Zamperini looked at his plane. The engineers counted over 700 holes and a huge amount of damage. Although Brooks died, the remainder owed their lives to 'Zamp', as his pilot called him. For gallantry in action that day, Zamperini was awarded the Oak Leaf Cluster and the Air Medal.

On 27 May 1943, while 'Superman' was being repaired, it was learned that a B-25 medium bomber had crashed in the sea 200 miles north of Palmyra and 800 miles south of their base in Hawaii. Zamperini was one of a crew of ten sent on the search mission. Another officer needing to go to Palmyra on business flew with them, as they would have to land there to refuel.

At first Louis Zamperini felt good about the idea of saving the B-25 crew. 'We'd recently saved a B-25 crew after they had ditched in the ocean … I had spotted them with the Zeiss binoculars I'd bought at the 1936 Olympics at Berlin.' The feeling of goodwill faded when they were told that the only Liberator available was an old model nicknamed 'Green Hornet'. It was full of 'gremlins', the airman's word for inexplicable mechanical failures. Normally it was only used for flights round Hawaii collecting lettuce, fresh vegetables, steak, and the like.

'Green Hornet' arrived in the area of the crashed plane. Suddenly her number one engine (left outboard) stopped and would not restart. Then number two engine (left inboard) also stopped. 'Green Hornet' was flying just below the cloud base at only 800 feet (240 metres) above the Pacific. Now all the power was in the two engines on the right wing—and that was not enough. The plane tipped over and crashed into the ocean, nose and left wing first. It spun over in half a cartwheel. Then there was a mighty explosion. The hapless 'Green Hornet' blew apart in a ball of flame.

Being a runner probably saved Zamperini's life. He could hold his breath longer than most people. He had practised this skill over and over again. When the crash occurred, Zamperini was on the right-hand side of the central part of the plane. The crewman to his left died instantly. Louis sucked in one last lungful of air and fought for freedom. He was dragged down and, worse still, became entangled in the Liberator's now useless control wires. Glancing through a nearby window, he saw two mangled bodies float past. Then he lost consciousness. For a reason he has never fully understood, he came to his senses on the surface. About three minutes had passed since 'Green Hornet' hit the water.

Silence followed the confusion. There was a cry for help.

Through a break in the smoke he saw a petrol tank with Lieutenant Russell Phillips (nicknamed Phil), his pilot, and Sergeant Francis McNamara, the tail gunner, clinging to it. Blood was pouring from the pilot's forehead. That was bad. It meant that sharks would be on the scene quickly. Zamperini saw two bright yellow life rafts that had been released and inflated automatically. He swam to them. After clawing his way aboard, he rowed to the other two men. They scrambled in.

The first task was to stop the bleeding from Phil's head. Zamperini pressed the carotid artery. The blood gushing from the triangular gash slowed. 'Mac, take off your T-shirt and hold it against his head,' he shouted.

After a while Phil said softly, 'Zamp, you're the captain now.'

The two rafts were lashed together. One served as Phil's 'hospital bed'. They would now be overdue at the base at Palmyra. Surely a search plane would be sent out fairly soon? The three men were shocked and overwhelmed as they realized that out of eleven men in 'Green Hornet', only three had survived.

Zamperini decided to check on what food and water they had. Suddenly McNamara screamed, 'We're gonna die. We're all gonna die!' The other two could hardly believe their ears.

'We're not going to die,' snapped Zamperini. 'We've rescued plenty of men and now they're out searching for us.' It was all so reasonable.

After four hours, Phil's bleeding stopped. Zamperini announced that they had six bars of chocolate and eight half-pint tins of water. It didn't seem a lot. Somehow that did not matter. After all, they were under ninety minutes' flying time from Palmyra. Surely they would be picked up quickly?

Phil, Mac and Zamperini were not churchgoing religious people. But now it seemed right to thank God. After all, the rest of the crew had died. Zamperini took the lead. The others joined in.

With a couple of sharks bumping the rafts with their noses, it seemed sensible to be on the side of whatever God there was.

After a week it was clear that they were drifting west. Their food was gone. Phil started to rally. Mac was a mental wreck. If he talked at all, the subject was death.

They were drifting inexorably towards enemy-held territory. At night it was extremely cold; during the day the heat was unbearable. Food became an obsession. Survival was achieved by killing albatrosses and catching fish. All were eaten raw. They even caught some small baby sharks and managed to consume their livers. Eating this sort of raw diet was so objectionable that it helped to dream of delicious home cooking. Occasional squalls of rain provided just enough water for survival.

On the twenty-seventh day they spotted a plane. They fired flares and put dye in the ocean. The plane's crew saw the three ragged, thin, bearded men waving their shirts. However, it was a Japanese aircraft. It flew over and machine-gunned the helpless men. Amazingly, they were unhurt.

During the thirty-third day the young, red-headed Francis McNamara died. Zamperini and Phillips recited the Lord's Prayer and slipped his body quietly into the ocean.

Feeling desperate, Zamperini prayed, 'Our Father in heaven, we are ignorant of your ways. We are here by no choice of our own and are completely helpless. Have mercy on us. Answer my prayers now, and I promise that if I get home … I'll seek you and serve you for the rest of my life.'

After forty-seven days on the raft, they had drifted 2,000 miles west towards the Marshall Islands.

Then they were rescued—by the Japanese.

Zamperini, who was five feet nine inches (1.75 metres), was reduced to a skeletal sixty-seven pounds (thirty kilos). Six weeks earlier he could have run a mile in just over four minutes and weighed 165 pounds (seventy-five kilos). On 13 July 1943 he could barely crawl out of the raft onto the Japanese patrol ship.

Wotje, Kwajalein, Ofuna, Omori and Naoestu are names that mean nothing to most people. To Zamperini they were the names of islands or places in Japan where he was held prisoner for two and a half years. In all the camps there were persistent beatings. Zamperini and the other prisoners were treated worse than caged animals. Every attempt was made to destroy their dignity as human beings. The only food ever offered was rice, supplemented infrequently by surreptitiously stolen items. The amounts were tiny. On one occasion he was used as a human guinea pig. The virus for dengue fever was injected into him. Two Japanese doctors recorded the terrible effects. 'At the time I wished I was dead,' he wrote later.

Zamperini was accurate when he assessed the guards as 'unintelligent brutes', so irrational that they could not be used as front-line soldiers. To him, the worst was a guard nicknamed 'The Bird' by the prisoners. 'The Bird' picked on Zamperini for no reason. Many a time he would knock him to the ground with his heavy steel belt-buckle or his kendo stick—similar to a baseball bat. Zamperini recorded that 'Compared with "The Bird", the other guards were gentlemen.' 'The Bird' was hated and feared because he derived personal satisfaction from causing unnecessary pain. As a result of this treatment some men lost the use of their minds and died in hopelessness. Zamperini, however, survived. He was sure that the disciplines involved in being an athlete helped him to cope with such horrendous experiences.

Zamperini's desire to kill 'The Bird' with his own hands was to be frustrated. Realizing that he would become a prisoner of the Americans when the war ended, the brutal guard fled into hiding on the Japanese mainland just a few days before the peace. In this way he escaped both vengeance and justice, although he was a Class 'A' war criminal.

The long-awaited day of release had come. Zamperini had been hungry for the greater part of three years. Ahead of him was food and care—as much food as he wanted! It must have sounded sheer bliss to all released prisoners.

During the Second World War, the US armed forces informed family members immediately when men and women were missing. However, after a year and a month, they would officially confirm death. As a result, in June 1944 Zamperini's parents had received the country's official notification of his death in action. It read:

IN GRATEFUL MEMORY OF
First Lieutenant Louis S. Zamperini, A.S. No.0–663341,
WHO DIED IN THE SERVICE OF HIS COUNTRY
in the Central Pacific Area, May 28, 1944.
HE STANDS IN THE UNBROKEN LINE OF PATRIOTS
WHO HAVE DARED TO DIE
THAT FREEDOM MIGHT LIVE, AND GROW,
AND INCREASE ITS BLESSINGS.
FREEDOM LIVES, AND THROUGH IT, HE LIVES—
IN A WAY THAT HUMBLES THE UNDERTAKINGS
OF MOST MEN.

Franklin D. Roosevelt,
President of the United States of America.

Contrary to this he was alive, though he looked ill and weighed only 110 pounds. Almost immediately after his release from the prison camp, he was officially informed that he was promoted to the rank of captain. A period of recuperation was followed by a rapturous homecoming. It was as if he had returned from the dead. At one banquet in his honour, he rashly announced that he aimed to qualify for the 1948 Olympics.

The Torrance homecoming celebrations went on for a long

time. Torrance Airfield had changed its name to Zamperini Field in his honour. He wallowed in the term 'war hero', though, as he said later, rather modestly, 'My only real accomplishment was staying alive.'

One thing completely went out of his mind. He forgot to thank God. The prayers offered on the raft and in prison camps were forgotten. There was no place in his life for God. As with most people not in trouble, he did not see what God had to do with anything in his life.

In early 1946 he met beautiful, nineteen-year-old Cynthia. Soon they were 'madly in love'. She asserted that all the men she knew were like boys compared to Louis. The proposal of marriage followed in ten days. There was $10,000 in back pay due to him, so in spite of vigorous opposition from Cynthia's well-to-do parents, they were married in May 1946.

What he did not tell Cynthia was the whole truth. When he returned from the Pacific, he brought with him an inward mountain of conflict and tension. Awake or asleep, 'The Bird' seemed to haunt him. Louis dreaded the nightmares that came every night. His solution was to stay up late and drink to excess in the hope that it would help. It didn't.

Nor did marriage cure the nightmares. Going from bar to bar, party to party, sometimes without Cynthia, he started to have alcoholic blackouts. His wife knew that he needed help, but every time it was suggested to him, he became extremely irritable with her. His back pay was slowly used up in get-rich-quick deals. Without exception, they failed. Steady jobs were for other men, not him.

One day he put a stopwatch in Cynthia's hand. Together they went to the local running track. The dream that he could qualify for the 1948 Olympics in London was still in his mind. Cynthia called out his times. They were too slow. He had to admit to Cynthia that a guard had once clubbed his legs. At least he had tried. Now they both knew that he would never again run competitively.

From this point life went downhill. Not even the birth of his daughter Cynthia, nicknamed 'Cissy', in January 1949 altered him. He would come home full of drink and find his wife in tears. They rowed. They made up. They rowed again, and made up again. One night he came in swaying and she said, 'If this keeps up, I may have to leave you.' Divorce was near. They both knew it.

It was September 1949. A pleasant young man rented the apartment next door. Zamperini, the non-practising Catholic, had one thing against the new neighbour. He was religious. Also, he was Protestant like Cynthia. Occasionally Cynthia expressed the desire to attend church and miss a party. Zamperini would have none of it.

The young man invited Cynthia to hear a preacher who had set up a large tent in downtown Los Angeles. 'I'd really like to go,' she told her husband. 'I'm curious.' When he heard that it was in a tent, he definitely determined not to attend, even out of curiosity. When he was younger he remembered seeing 'Holy Rollers'. With his boyhood companions he had lifted the tent flap and watched the antics of these religious fanatics. They were making a spectacle of themselves—rolling in the dust and screaming in frenzy. Some were on their backs. They raised their hands and feet upwards 'to the Lord'.

When he told the Catholic priest, he was warned to stay away. 'They're demon-possessed,' the priest asserted. Perhaps they were.

So Cynthia went alone to the big tent. That night Zamperini went to a party, convinced that the divorce would go ahead, no matter what he did. When he returned she actually smiled at him.

'What's going on?' he asked, sensing something had happened.

'I went to hear Reverend Billy Graham,' she replied.

'And?' he probed, tensing himself up for a fight.

She answered, 'I've received Christ as my Saviour.' At first he said nothing, but then thought she was too smart to be taken in by nonsense like this. She smiled again. Louis went to bed baffled.

The next morning she was as cheerful as the previous evening. Zamperini wouldn't give way. 'I don't understand it and I don't like it,' was all he could say.

She replied perceptively, 'You don't understand it because you don't understand yourself.'

At this time the young man from next door visited them and started talking about religion. During the conversation Zamperini remarked, 'I don't understand the Bible.'

The neighbour said, 'You must receive God's Spirit into your heart before you can really understand the Bible.' That comment meant nothing at all to Zamperini.

Later, Cynthia asked Louis again if he would go with her to the tent meeting. Reluctantly, he gave way. He would go just once.

The notice outside the tent announced that there were 6,000 free seats. Zamperini looked at the picture of the young Billy Graham. At least he didn't look like a 'Holy Roller'. From the start of the service Zamperini knew that he would not be influenced. In his early preaching meetings—and this was the first—Billy Graham sounded like a machine gun shooting out strings of Bible texts like bullets. However, he didn't scream and shout. No, he definitely was not a 'Holy Roller'. But in a message about sin and evil, why did it seem that he was directing his remarks directly at the reluctant Zamperini?

This is what thirty-two-year-old Zamperini heard: 'There is not a righteous man on earth who does what is right and never sins. For all have sinned and come short of the glory of God.' Zamperini felt annoyed. Was this preacher saying that good deeds do not get you to heaven? Well, Graham was wrong. Zamperini thought about some of the kind and decent things he had done. He could afford to let the man rave on.

Next he heard: 'He saved us, not because of righteous things we have done, but because of his mercy.' It was almost as if he was hearing the Bible's response to his thoughts.

Then came: 'For God so loved the world that he gave his only begotten Son that whoever believes in him should not perish but have everlasting life.' Hearing that, he grabbed Cynthia's arm, pulled her up out of the seat and almost ran out of the tent.

That night he could not sleep. One verse that had been quoted was like an unwelcome intruder: 'Man is destined to die once, and after that to face judgement' (Hebrews 9:27). When sleep eventually came, so did the nightmares. There was Satan in hell, swinging a wide belt with its heavy buckle. The face of Satan was that of the sardonic, grinning 'Bird'.

During the following days Zamperini brooded. Cynthia urged a return to the tent. Eventually he consented to a repeat visit. 'I'll go under one condition,' he told her, 'and that is that you leave with me whenever I ask you.'

'I promise,' returned his wife.

When Graham spoke it was all about the emptiness of material wealth and its inability to buy salvation—which is a free gift from God. Then followed the Bible verses which say, 'What good is it for a man to gain the whole world, yet forfeit his soul? Or what can a man give in exchange for his soul?' (Mark 8:36–37). Zamperini thought of his get-rich-quick- methods of taking unwise chances with his precious back pay. He squirmed in his seat as Graham quoted: 'For it is by grace you have been saved, through faith—and this not from yourselves, it is the gift of God—not by works, so that no one can boast' (Ephesians 2:8–9). That angered Zamperini.

Graham continued: 'God commands you to repent of your sins and then completely surrender your life to Christ and follow him.' Zamperini thought, 'Surrender? Not for me. All I wanted to surrender to was the overwhelming desire to escape from the tent. I needed a drink.'

As he was about to get up, Graham read two more Bible verses which stunned him: 'God has given us eternal life, and this life is in his Son. He who has the Son has life; he who does not have the Son of God does not have life' (1 John 5:11–12). Zamperini had never denied that Jesus was the Son of God, but he knew that he did not have the Son of God *in* his life—not in the spiritual sense that the preacher meant.

Zamperini felt as if a weight was pressing on his chest. His throat tightened. He gasped for air. He dropped to his knees in the tent and, for the first time in his life, truly humbled himself before God. Zamperini repented and asked the Lord to forgive him for his sin and his godless life. He was particularly conscious of not having kept the promises he had made during the war.

The Bible says, 'Everyone who calls on the name of the Lord will be saved' (Romans 10:13). Zamperini took God at his word, begged for his pardon and put his faith in Christ. He waited. True to his promise, the Lord came into his heart and life. Zamperini later recalled how remarkable that moment was. He said, 'It was the most realistic experience I'd ever had. I am not sure what I expected; perhaps my life or my sins or a great white light would flash before my eyes; perhaps I'd feel a shock like being hit by a bolt of lightning. Instead, I felt no tremendous sensation, just an enveloping calm that let me know that I had come to Christ and he had come to me.'

'I'm through with my past life,' he told Cynthia. She smiled, realizing that a miracle had taken place.

The next morning he woke up and realized that for once he hadn't had a nightmare about 'The Bird'. From that time the nightmares ceased permanently. It was as if a doctor had cut out the hating part of his brain. That morning Zamperini took a half-mile walk to Barnsdale Park. In his pocket was the New Testament that all servicemen were given on the orders of

President Roosevelt. He had tried to read it before, but did not understand it.

In the park, he sat down under a tree. Chin on chest, he prayed. He felt the need to be absolutely alone. The spiritual struggle was not over. Feelings of uncertainty plagued him. Despondency was still a problem. He opened the book at the Gospel of John. The reading began with: 'In the beginning was the Word, and the Word was with God, and the Word was God ...'

For the first time, the story of Christ began to make sense. Oblivious to people who passed by, he read on in the Gospel of John. It took him all morning to reach the nineteenth chapter. That was about the crucifixion of Jesus. As he read, he began to weep. It crossed his mind that he had never cried about anything for years—not even when tortured or on the life raft. Up to this moment the Bible had been a mystery to him. Now he understood it. He knew that he was experiencing the power and presence of God's Spirit.

As his inner battle came to a conclusion, he realized that God was working directly in his life for his own good. Reflecting on this later, Zamperini wrote, 'The Lord had seen to it that I'd made it through every life-threatening situation, and lost in every business venture, because that was what brought me to the tent. Now I knew that God had prepared me for this moment. Otherwise I would never have known Christ.'

Zamperini made a radical decision to break with his old lifestyle. There were numerous bottles of alcohol in the house. One by one he poured the contents into the sink. Next he threw his cigarettes into the bin. Cynthia watched all this with amazement. That was the moment at which she was convinced that he had undergone a real conversion to Christ. 'Now I am not going to get a divorce,' she declared.

Most of his 'friends' on the party and drinks circuit didn't think his new-found faith would last. Some thought he wanted publicity. Time proved all of them wrong.

Louis Zamperini and Cynthia started a new life together. This included regular family prayers night and morning. Of course, his problems did not entirely vanish after his radical spiritual experience. The Bible never promises a life free from difficulties, but it does promise that God is with the believer whatever the circumstances. The periods of depression were less frequent. A visit to the Veterans' Employment Service set him looking for honest work. From now on their lives were consciously in God's hands. Where would it lead?

After he left Japan at the end of the war, *Time* magazine had published an article about him in which he said, 'I'd rather be dead than return to that country.' In 1950 he began to feel burdened by the shadows of the past. The ultimate test of his faith, the proof that it was real, would be to face the guards he quite naturally hated, look them in the face, and see if he could forgive them from his heart.

With Cynthia's blessing he returned. It was October 1950. Zamperini arrived at Tokyo's drab airport. Would resentment well up inside him? Was his spiritual experience authentic? Most of the war-crimes trials were over. It was well known that 850 of the worst of those who perpetrated atrocities were held in Sugamo Prison. By now Zamperini was used to public speaking. Giving his testimony and preaching now constituted a primary calling. As he stood before the prisoners, he wondered if any would recognize him. After all, his face was older and fuller. His message, interpreted by missionary Fred Jarvis, never carried so much conviction. Inside he wanted these men to find new life, to be spiritually reborn as he had been. It was all made clear: he did not represent the American authorities; if they showed any interest in the gospel, it would not reduce their sentences.

The colonel in charge of Sugamo joined Zamperini on the

platform when he had finished speaking and said, 'Those of you who were Louis' guards may come forward if you wish. He would like to speak with you.' As he waited, men walked slowly down the aisles and faces emerged from the mists of memory. The colonel ushered them all into a small room. Instinctively, without prior thought, Zamperini threw his arms round each of them. They were plainly startled by his genuine affection. Those Japanese guards knew what they had done. With the greetings over, he explained the gospel of forgiveness again. Some believed. Some said they did not understand. Some rejected the message. Most accepted New Testaments supplied by the Gideons.

Leaving the grey prison, Zamperini turned to his companion and said, 'I am a happy man, Fred.' Inside his heart he was exultant. He felt that he had done the right thing both for the prisoners and himself. The one regret that he had was that the twenty-third most wanted war criminal, Matsuhiro Watanabe, 'The Bird', was not there. To Zamperini 'The Bird' was now just one more lost soul. He was more to be pitied than hated.

When Zamperini landed back at Los Angeles, there was no welcoming party except his wife and child. Back at home he reflected over recent events. Parts of his life were now over: the juvenile delinquency, the phase as an Olympic track star, the Air Force bombardier, the time on the raft, being a prisoner of war, the drinking, the nightmares, the get-rich-quick deals and the constant unhappiness. It was as if he had passed a test about the reality of his own forgiveness. He was now ready to move on.

His faith developed and deepened. Probably at first it was man-centred. It was as if *he* had made a decision. 'I believe what the Bible says,' he recorded: '"Many are called but few are chosen."' On reflection he knew that election and grace came first. The family now settled into the membership and ministry of First Presbyterian Church, Hollywood.

Soon after his return from Japan, he received the chance to

make some honest money. An organization employed lecturers who travelled around the country giving talks on a regular- salary basis. 'Your story is thrilling,' he was told. 'You think it is all right for your audiences?' Zamperini enquired. The payment would be $50,000 a year with a seven-year contract. 'What happens after seven years?' Zamperini asked. The answer was: 'We start all over again.' He was amazed—such a large salary for so little effort! His mind contemplated the good he could do with that sort of money. Then came the catch. He would have to make some minor changes. He could talk freely about God, but they said he couldn't mention Christ by name. Zamperini's response may sound dogmatic to some people: 'The least I can do for Christ is to turn down your offer. If I can't mention Christ, I can't speak at all. I don't want your contract.'

He telephoned Cynthia and told her about the offer. Without hesitation, she supported his decision.

In 1954 the TV programme *This Is Your Life* was very popular in America. The producers surprised him. Enticed into a studio, he was startled to meet his parents, his brother and sisters, together with Cynthia and their two children, Cissy and Luke. In addition, the producers had gathered together his pilot Russell Phillips, who had shared forty-seven days on the raft with him, and Jesse Owens, the great Olympic athlete, along with other people such as his first track coach.

He became Youth Director at the Hollywood Church. Having been a troubled teenager himself, he was burdened about the street gangs of Los Angeles. The city authorities sent hundreds of young men to him. They were committing every crime in the book. Zamperini would ask the young men, 'Why did you rob that petrol station?' 'Why did you start on marijuana?' 'Why did you beat up the old person?' In their replies he discerned a common element: 'I did it for kicks.' 'I did it for laughs.' 'I did it for thrills.' Underneath he knew that the real problem was inborn evil. As a result he began a series of what were called Victory Boys' Camps. They worked like a dream. He and his helpers set up a programme of mountaineering, glacier climbing, skiing, survival, rescue, and sports of all sorts. They were like Outward Bound courses, with the difference that they included attendance at chapel in the morning and a devotional epilogue at night. A great many unruly young men became Christians. Zamperini's own life had been influenced by sport, so that was the approach he used. It worked.

Zamperini was among those who ran with the Olympic torch in the 1984 Summer Games in Los Angeles. In 1996 he carried the Olympic torch again in Atlanta. For his eighty-first birthday, he ran a kilometre leg with the 1998 Olympic torch at the Winter Olympics at Nagano in Japan. While he was in Nagano 'The Bird' was tracked down by a reporter. Probably too embarrassed, he refused to see Zamperini. However, the thought of 'The Bird' escaping scot-free did not cause Zamperini any bitterness. He forgave because he understood what God's forgiveness had done for him.

In later years, Zamperini ran a programme for retired people at the Hollywood Church. This included a lunch club, a nutrition programme and outdoor activities. Aged eighty-seven, he still remained active in sport, taking a run every day. Sometimes he would fly his old single-engine ex-military plane at the airfield bearing his name. During air shows he even gave aerobatic displays. He remained a youth counsellor at his church. When interviewed, he would say that the war took ten years off his life. By sensible healthy living he attempted to retrieve the lost years. As a result, he can still lead an active life in the service of the Lord when aged eighty-nine, as he described in a telephone conversation with the author.

Cynthia also had a deep faith. She sold many paintings, and wrote three novels which were well reviewed. Throughout the fifty-five years of their marriage, she supported and encouraged

Louis in all he did. She died of cancer in February 2001. Louis has never lost the absolute certainty that he will see her again.

In 2003 his stirring memoir *Devil at my Heels* was rewritten and updated. Without exception, it received excellent reviews. The following year, the University of Southern California called the entrance to its track stadium the Louis Zamperini Plaza.

Also in 2004 he gave an interview to a journalist. It was displayed on the Internet, and at the end he expresses some of his most basic convictions. They are identical to the faith he expressed to the writer of this account: 'I'm a great believer, and I believe it with all my heart, that all things work together for good for those who love the Lord, and who are called according to his purpose. Christ told us in the Scriptures, "I am the way, I am the truth, and I am the life. Whoever comes to me I will never drive away." Christ is the way to God. I believe our eternal life starts now by faith in Jesus Christ. That is the strength we live by, and death no longer has a sting—not to the Christian.'

Louis Zamperini died on 2 July 2014 at the age of ninety–seven.

More information on Louis Zamperini

E. P. Dutton & Co. of New York published *Devil at my Heels*, by Louis Zamperini with Helen Itria, in 1956. The book tells his story up to that date.

After that there were occasional interviews and articles about him. Author Curtis Mitchell published a book that includes a life story and a lengthy interview about Zamperini's youth work. Occasional TV documentaries were also made. Particularly notable is the DVD produced by World Wide Films in which Louis tells his own story. This includes some perceptive self-analysis. The DVD, which lasts thirty-seven minutes, is called *Zamperini—Still Carrying the Torch*. There are several Internet suppliers of this 1992 production.

The existence of the Internet has allowed a lot of interviews and short accounts of his life to be displayed. An outstanding one is by the World Olympians Association.

Almost all of this material, if gathered together, would provide the substance of a book about him. I have consulted everything available and included relevant material not covered in the new edition of *Devil at my Heels* published in 2003. Louis Zamperini wrote this with David Rensin. It is published by William Morrow, an imprint of HarperCollins in America. Most UK bookshops do not regularly stock the title. As a result, Louis sent me some photographs to accompany this story in the hope that reading it would encourage some people outside the US to read his own account by ordering the 2003 edition of *Devil at my Heels*. It is my hope that this brief account may lead some to procure that book.

In 2010 Laura Hillenbrand wrote another biography about Louis Zamperini. It is called *Unbroken*, and is the basis of a Hollywood film of the same name, directed by Angelina Jolie.

2

Paul Schneider

German opponent of Hitler

To be a Nazi and to be a German patriot had become the same thing for most people in the land. Paul Schneider was a patriotic German. His hard-won war medal proved that he would fight for his country, but now he was opposing a military-backed dictatorship.

2

Paul Schneider

Throughout 1915 the First World War raged in both western and eastern Europe. In the German onslaught in the east against Russia, Paul Robert Schneider, an eighteen-year-old German soldier, received a serious wound in the stomach. For his bravery he was awarded the Iron Cross.

After surgery and recovery from it, Paul Schneider fought in the artillery against Britain and France. His courage did not go unrecognized. By the end of the war he had risen to the rank of lieutenant. At about the same time another German soldier ended the war as a corporal. His name was Adolf Hitler.

Adolf Hitler is now regarded as one of the most evil men who has ever lived. For twelve years, from 1933 to 1945, his political party, the National Socialists, or Nazis, dominated the life of Germany. For many years after 1933 his following among the German people was almost complete. Cheering crowds greeted him with rapturous enthusiasm whenever he appeared in public. He was idolized like a god. His power was so great that he led his people into an aggressive war in which millions died. His legacy to the country he ruled as a dictator was ruin and shame.

During those fateful years, the opposition to Hitler within Germany was so small that it was crushed with ease. Those who openly protested against Nazi ideology or policies paid a heavy price. The great scientist Einstein pointed out the origins of the most effective resistance: 'Only the church stood squarely across the path of Hitler's campaign to suppress truth ... it had the courage to stand for intellectual truth and moral freedom.'[1]

When Germany was defeated in 1918, Paul Schneider decided to give up his original plan to be a physician. His father, Gustav-Adolph, was a pastor in the German Evangelische Reformierte Kirche, a church that is Presbyterian in organization and belief. Paul's decision to study theology at this time probably had a great deal to do with the influence of his family background.

It is not surprising that the years immediately after the war were a time of mental turmoil for him. Since schooldays he had been taught the critical view of the Bible. This held that it was full of mistakes and could not be trusted. He was also troubled by the appeal of communism and socialism. As a German, he did not like the parts of the Treaty of Versailles that allegedly humiliated his country. He struggled spiritually, yet it was clear to him that, unless people's hearts were changed, a new tyranny would merely replace an old one like that of the Kaiser.

Just before Christmas in 1921, as his theological studies began, his spiritual struggles came to an end. He rejected his positive view of human nature, which he realized was derived from nineteenth-century optimism. The Reformers Luther and Calvin were right: man is a sinner in need of redemption. The Bible is not just religious folklore; it is the Word of God. Gretel, the young lady who was to become his wife, recorded: 'Eternal life entered his soul and he was filled with great joy.'[2]

From his diaries and letters we know that he experienced a

definite personal conversion to Christ. Now he had a message to preach: the biblical gospel that salvation is by repentance and faith in the crucified and risen Christ. He could see the Reformation confessions of his church not just as historical documents but also as statements of his faith. Later on, when in prison, he asked his wife to let him have the *Belgic Confession* and the *Heidelberg Catechism* to study alongside his Bible. Paul Schneider had become a Reformed evangelical Christian.

During the demanding preparation to be a pastor, he felt the need to experience the life of an ordinary workingman. An uncle heard of his plan to work in a factory for a while, and offered him a comfortable, well-paid job. But he did not want a 'soft' job. So throughout most of 1922 Paul Schneider became part of a gang of workers at a blast furnace near Dortmund. He said that he needed to understand the demands of the daily grind such men face. They

Paul Schneider and Margarete Dieterich (usually known as Gretel), engagement photograph, 22 October 1922

showed him their respect and on the day he left said, 'You are one of us. Try to stay like that.'[3] He did.

The years before his ordination were filled with study at university and theological college. For nine months up to July 1924 he worked for the Berlin City Mission, becoming acquainted with poor and wretched men and women, some of them addicted to alcohol and drugs.

Ordination followed in 1925. For a time he was an assistant pastor in Essen. In 1926 his father suffered a stroke while preaching and died three days later. His father's church at Hochelheim unanimously called Paul to succeed him as pastor. He had been married less than a month when he was installed as pastor in September 1926. His first sermon was based on 2 Timothy 3:14–17, the heart of which declares that all Scripture is God-breathed, which means that it is without error—that is, infallible. The choice of this passage indicates his belief in the authority of the Bible alone. He was Reformed in his faith and his ministry was Bible-based. All surviving accounts indicate that he was a bold and powerful preacher.

He also had a real loving concern for the people. There are descriptions in existence of the sick listening for the distinctive whine of his motorcycle on his way to visit them. Gretel, his wife, records that in their dying moments some testified that Paul Schneider was the one used by God to bring peace through leading them to faith in Christ.

In Gretel's memoir of Paul there is another story from that period. A young epileptic had a very severe attack, which went on for three days and nights. In spite of strong narcotics, nobody could give him rest. Then Paul Schneider arrived. He prayed for the helpless boy and spoke quietly to him. Peace came and the boy fell asleep. Later Schneider returned once more at just the right moment. 'I knew I was needed here,' he said as he arrived. Just before the boy died peacefully in Paul's arms, he said clearly,

'I thank you all for everything, but that I can die at peace with my God and with no fear of the grave, I thank our pastor.' The pastor knew where the power came from. His diary says, 'I am utterly dependent on the grace of God alone.'[4]

Paul Schneider was an example of a minister who was rarely off duty. His work was his life. We see him trying to win young people to Christ by playing sports or going on rambles with them. Older folk working in the fields would find him joining the work of harvesting or haymaking. He built up his relationships with the local people. Yet within his congregation he believed in applying biblical church discipline to a few who had scandalous lifestyles and came to the Lord's Table as though they were doing nothing wrong.

On 30 January 1933 Hitler came to power, and life in Germany began to change. Of the one thousand people in Schneider's rural Rhineland parish of Hochelheim, half freely voted for the Nazis. Nevertheless, from an early stage of Nazi rule, Paul Schneider spoke out against wrong policies and actions. He would never use the greeting, 'Heil Hitler', quite reasonably considering it a form of idolatry.

So-called 'Christians' who accepted Nazism were known as 'German Christians'. Schneider would have nothing to do with them because they accepted Hitler's anti-Semitic policies. Eventually Paul Schneider put some criticisms of Nazism on his church bulletin board and was forced to account for what he said to a 'German Christian' leader. This man was dressed in Nazi uniform and had a huge cross dangling on his chest. Paul could see that these people were trying to force the church to adopt Nazi ideas. Sadly, the elders of the Hochelheim Church would not support him in his stand. As a result, he was forced to take a new pastorate with two churches, one in Dickenschied and the other nearby in Womrath.

Paul Schneider was installed as minister in May 1934, at the age of thirty-six. He had been in his new pastorate for only a few weeks when faithful men who thought as he did issued the Barmen Declaration. Part of the wording of this declaration defiantly asserted: 'Jesus Christ, as he is attested for us in Holy Scripture, is the one Word of God which we have to hear and which we have to trust and obey in life and in death.'[5]

Just over a month after he began his new ministry a completely unexpected incident occurred. Tuesday, 12 June, dawned as just another beautiful early summer day in rural Rhineland. As Schneider travelled to nearby Gemünden to stand in for another pastor at a funeral service, he had no idea of the trouble that lay ahead.

Wearing his simple black clerical robe, Paul Schneider walked in front of the bearers of the coffin towards the open grave. Ahead of him could be seen a parade of the Hitler Youth organization with bands and flags. He recalled that the dead seventeen-year-old youth had told him that he was the first young man in Gemünden to join the Hitler Youth. Paul conducted the graveside service, but before the committal and without asking permission, the local Nazi leader, Heinrich Nadig, spoke at some length and then asserted: 'Comrade Karl Moog, you have now been enlisted in Horst Wessel's battalion in heaven.'[6]

As Paul stepped forward to pronounce the benediction, he knew that something must be said to make it clear to the hundreds of youthful Nazis that Horst Wessel was not part of a Christian burial. As reasonably as he could, he explained the truth of the gospel and rejected the idea that there is a Horst Wessel group in heaven.

The local Nazi leader then approached the coffin and half addressing the crowd and half addressing the dead youth, he insisted: 'Comrade, whatever they say, you are now enlisted in Horst Wessel's battalion.'[7] Paul Schneider protested and reminded

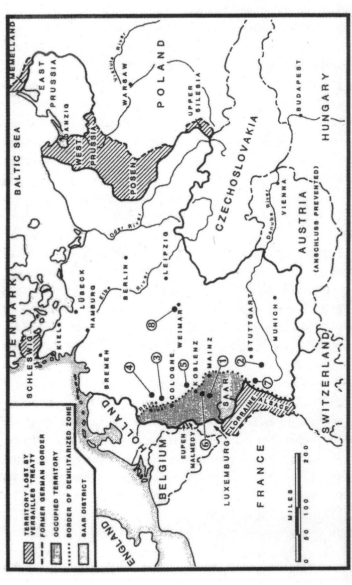

1 = Pferdsfeld 2 = Tübingen 3 = Dortmund 4 = Soest 5 = Hochelheim/Dornholzhausen 6 = Dickenschied/Womrath 7 = Baden Baden 8 = Buchenwald Map to show places associated with the life of Paul Schneider

the Nazi leader that he was at a church service. The Nazi stormed away and the parade broke up.

The day after the funeral Schneider was arrested and imprisoned for a week. On his release he was given a strong warning to stop opposing the wishes of the state.

What was the Nazi thinking in all this? They had revived old pagan legends, one being the Viking myth that at death the individual joins other departed warriors. They idolized various folk heroes. Horst Wessel was a Nazi who had been shot in a street fight with political enemies in 1930. He became a Nazi folk hero, and was glorified as a martyr. The Horst Wessel song, full of pagan sentiments, was often sung at rallies when Hitler was present.

When the pastor made his graveside protest against Nazi ideology, he was holding to the right of the church to defend the purity of Christian truth. While in prison he informed the Nazi officials that he did not intend to be antagonistic to the state, but if there was to be harmony between church and state, the Nazis should respect the rights of the church to maintain the truth of the gospel. He had embarked, single-handed for all he knew, on a collision course with an increasingly dominant police state.

During the winter of 1935–36 the Nazis rebuked Paul Schneider on twelve occasions. They resented the fact that faithful Christians had organized themselves into the 'Confessing Church'. This body issued a statement that was intended to be read openly in faithful gospel churches. The Gestapo, the State Secret Police, visited Paul and put pressure on him to sign a document agreeing not to read it publicly. True to his principles, he refused. For that, he was imprisoned for four days.

Paul Schneider also resisted the pressure that was put on Christian youth movements to integrate into the Hitler Youth. Somebody reported him for not using the 'Heil Hitler' salute at his confirmation classes. He considered the salute as idolatry and would not use it on principle. Schneider particularly loathed the hate propaganda against the Jews. His church had an organization that was a mission to German Jews. When he went ahead with his usual collection for the Mission to the Jews, Nazi feelings were inflamed against him. Later this Nazi anti-Semitism would lead to the Holocaust, an undisguised attempt at total genocide.

In the early hours of 7 March 1936 Hitler ordered German troops to occupy the Rhineland. One of the provisions of the Treaty of Versailles was that part of the Rhineland was to be demilitarized. By sending German soldiers to seize it back, Hitler was openly defying the peace treaty. The world held its breath. Rather than cause another war, Hitler was allowed to win. He was jubilant at his success. Most Germans agreed with him. Many historians now think that if the Allies had resisted Hitler over the Rhineland incident, he might have acted differently when it came to seizing lands that were not German territory.

The Nazis organized a ballot supposedly to indicate whether German citizens approved of Hitler's illegal action. The ballot paper had no place to say 'No', so the inevitable result was ninety-nine per cent in favour of Hitler. On the day of the vote, Nazi police visited Paul and Gretel to try to persuade them to vote. Their decision not to vote was one more major accusation that was levelled against the rebel pastor.

On Sunday morning a few days later, the Schneiders awoke to find a message in large red letters daubed on the front of their house: 'He did not vote. Fatherland, people, what do you say to that?' Spontaneously, members of his congregation gathered cleaning materials and wiped away the Nazi response to their pastor.

To be a Nazi and to be a German patriot had become the same thing for most people in the land. Paul Schneider was a patriotic German. His hard-won war medal proved that he would fight for his country, but now he was opposing a military-backed dictatorship. Trade unions had been abolished. The media were in the grip of the Nazi party. Textbooks were rewritten. Human biology was dominated by the Nazi belief that some races were 'higher' and that they would eliminate 'lower' races by force. By the time of the vote, Hitler had supreme power. He was Fuehrer (Leader) of the whole nation and all the armed forces. There was a lot of evidence to support what Paul Schneider said at the time: 'National Socialism becomes more obviously opposed to biblical Christianity every day.'[8]

The sermons he preached were powerful. Often they included passages like this: 'Do not deceive yourselves, you cannot participate in Jesus' glory and victory unless you, for his sake, take up the holy cross and go with him along the path of suffering and death.'[9]

By the summer of 1936 the Schneiders had a family of four boys and a girl—and their education intensified his troubles. Both his churches had single-class church schools attached to them. The two teachers had joined the Nazi party and used their positions to indoctrinate the children. Paul Schneider tried to intervene. After all, they were church-based schools, and he was the father of five of the pupils.

As a result, Nazi police searched his house. Papers and sermon notes were taken away and not returned. Doubtless this was because some of his sermons contained references to ways in which Nazism and the Bible were in disagreement. The Gestapo dossier of his opposition to Nazi beliefs and policies grew ever bigger.

On most days he was out and about using his motorcycle for pastoral visits. One evening in March 1937, he was returning home after taking a confirmation class at Womrath. He did not arrive at the expected time. Gretel received the news that in the dense fog he had collided with an unlit farm trailer carelessly parked on the road. His left leg was broken in three places and had to be put in a plaster cast. He was kept in hospital.

A little while later his sixth child was born. Paul wrote a

Gretel Schneider with her six children

poem, as he often did to celebrate important events. Interestingly, they named the child Ernst Wilhelm, the names of two of Gretel's brothers killed while fighting the British at the Battle of the Somme in 1916.

On 31 May 1937 two Gestapo agents burst into his study and arrested him. His general health was not good because his leg had only been out of plaster for a few days. They gave him no time to pack any belongings. Gretel was informed that he would be taken to nearby Koblenz for questioning.

He was held in an underground cell. There was no charge, no questioning and no trial. The reason given for his arrest was that he was a danger to public order. In the world of the Gestapo he became 'Prisoner Schneider', not 'Pastor Schneider'. In an attempt to intimidate him, he was treated like a common criminal by having his photograph taken from every angle and his fingerprints recorded. Eventually he was allowed to write to Gretel. She was urged not to worry about him because 'All is in God's hands and he will use the matter …' Although he would be present only in spirit, he urged Gretel to go ahead with the baptism of their sixth child. Another long poem celebrated the birth of the child and the baptism.

After eight weeks he was released. However, there was a condition. He must accept an expulsion order from the Rhineland.

Paul made it absolutely clear that he could not accept the legality of such an order that would separate him from his home and his churches. After all, there had been no trial, just the so-called 'law' of the Gestapo. To make their point, the Nazis bundled him into a car, drove him fifty miles to Wiesbaden, just over the Rhineland border, and left him there. To make *his* point Paul put the illegal banishment papers in a rubbish bin and caught the first train home. He was taking a big risk.

When he arrived home he looked ill; he was exhausted and his leg needed medical attention. Friends persuaded him to go for treatment and convalescence at Baden Baden, which lay outside the Rhineland. Here he was safe. Outwardly it appeared that he accepted the banishment order.

After a week Gretel joined him. Her hope was that he would give in to the Gestapo and find a church outside the Rhineland. Paul, however, had made a firm decision while in the Gestapo prison at Koblenz. He would resist unjustified bullying. With questioning in her mind, Gretel reminded him that if he went back to his Dickenschied pulpit, he would be rearrested. Paul quoted some words from a Bible verse to her. They came from Judges 5:18 and said, translated literally, 'Zebulun ... and Naphtali ... risked their lives to the point of death.' Hearing him quote this, Gretel hung her head in despair. Her voice quivered as she asked, 'Paul, don't you think about the children and me? Paul, don't you love us?'

Paul's eyes filled with tears. With powerful arms he hugged Gretel to his chest. 'My darling', he sobbed, 'I have never loved you or the children more than on that night of decision. I wept for you.'[10] With those words, spoken with such deep emotion, pathos and conviction, Gretel knew that her only choice was to identify herself with her husband.

It was 5 October 1937, Harvest Festival Sunday. Paul Schneider returned to Dickenschied. His family and friends were overjoyed to see him. However, the well-informed people knew he was taking a risk. He preached at Dickenschied in the morning on Psalm 145:15–21. Did he have any idea that it would be his last pulpit message—that the very act of preaching in his own church would lead to the loss of all he held dear? He went by car to Womrath to take the evening service. Police cars with flashing lights blocked the road. As he was arrested, he called out to Gretel: 'Tell the church that I am and shall remain the pastor of Dickenschied and Womrath.'[11] Gretel just had time to push a Bible into his pocket.

He was held for some time in the Koblenz prison, constantly being urged to sign a document agreeing to banishment. 'What do you do all day?' asked Gretel in one letter. His answer was: 'I am a pupil in the school of God's Word.'[12]

Behind the scenes the faithful church, the 'Confessing Church', was facing enforced closure of all its work. It did not have the power to help Paul Schneider, one of its most distinguished members. Its best-known leader, Martin Niemöller, a Lutheran pastor who had once captained a First World War U-boat, was himself in prison. Schneider and Niemöller shared the dubious distinction of being Hitler's 'personal prisoners', meaning that he had personally signed the order to silence them. The official reason given by the Nazis for suspending anyone's liberty was always 'to defend the state'. Effectively, the Gestapo had absolute power about who could be arrested, and what to do with protesters. Those in prison paid for their own captivity by the confiscation of all assets. It was a good thing Paul lived in a house he did not own. Even the garden had been purchased in Gretel's name only.

On 25 November 1937 Paul Schneider was taken to Buchenwald Concentration Camp near Weimar, about 200 miles from his home at Dickenschied. Gretel and the children said a final farewell. The image of her husband smiling and waving as he was driven away stayed forever in Gretel's mind.

Karl Koch, the Nazi in charge of the camp, had total power over the inmates. The guards constantly taunted Schneider. As one man said, 'The walls of his prison were made of paper.'[13] In other words, if he would agree to sign a document relinquishing care of his churches and accept banishment, he could go free. Just consider the immense pressure on him to sign and go back to his family!

From the beginning he had no privileges. Like the others, he worked sixteen-hour shifts. Constantly he maintained his Christian witness. He fasted every Friday and gave his meagre food ration to others.

20 April 1938 was Hitler's forty-ninth birthday. To honour him, the prisoners were lined up and ordered to remove their berets and venerate the Nazi swastika flag. As one man the parade whipped off its headgear. The guards noticed the solitary figure who would not bow to the swastika—Paul Schneider. For this he was viciously struck twenty-five times with an oxhide whip. His bleeding body was left in solitary confinement. Here he stayed for the next fifteen months. The cell was four feet wide and ten feet long (1.2 metres by 3 metres). There was no furniture, no electric light, and all he ever had to eat was bread and water. Before long he became a broken skeleton. His clothes became rags and his body crawled with vermin. Nor was he allowed a Bible.

On the morning of Sunday, 28 August 1938, Paul Schneider preached through the bars of his cell to men lined up for the 06.30 roll call. Survivors recorded what he said: 'Our Lord Jesus Christ came into the world to save us from our sins. If we have faith in him, we are put right with God. We need not fear what man may do to us because we, through Christ, belong to the kingdom of God … Our Lord Jesus Christ who died for us has promised that we, by faith in him, may participate in his resurrection. He said, "I am the resurrection and the life. He that believes in me shall

A framed copy of this photograph of Paul Schneider hangs in the cell he once occupied at Buchenwald.

never die." Accept the Lord Jesus as your Saviour, and God will receive you as his child …'[14]

After two minutes guards rushed into his cell and pulled him away from the bars of the window. For this message he was once again tied to a rack and suffered another twenty-five strokes of the whip. Schneider's response to a friend was: 'Somebody has to preach God's Word in this hell.'[15]

In January 1939 two prisoners who tried to escape were hanged in front of the assembled inmates. Paul Schneider called out through his cell window: 'In the name of Jesus Christ, I witness against the murder of these prisoners …'[16] The response was another twenty-five lashes.

A guard said to him, 'If we released you, what would you do?'[17] Seeing in his mind's eye the image of two men hanging on the gallows, Paul replied, 'I would go to Weimar [the nearest town] and the first kerbstone would become a pulpit from which I would denounce the brutal crimes committed here.'[18] For saying that, he was suspended by his wrists from the window bars, with his feet off the floor, for hours.

He continued his brief messages through the cell window. One prisoner recalled Paul Schneider preaching the message of new life in Christ on Easter Day 1939. Another who survived later commented: 'In my estimation he was the only man in Germany who, overcoming all human fear, so consciously took on himself the cross of Christ even to death.'[19] Every time he preached from his bunker, his tortures increased, but his faith in the Lord grew stronger.

Finally, on 18 July 1939, the starved, beaten, bleeding Paul Schneider died when the camp doctor injected a massive overdose of strophanthin. Paul was forty-one years old. Gretel became a widow at the age of thirty-five.

Dietrich Bonhoeffer, a definite opponent of the Nazis, received the news of Schneider's death in 1939. At the time he was staying in London with his sister Sabine. The Christian writer and theologian said to his nieces and nephews, 'Listen children. You must never forget the name of Pastor Paul Schneider. He is our first martyr.'[20] (Bonhoeffer himself later returned to Germany and was hanged by the Nazis in 1945.)

The telegram to Gretel from the Buchenwald commandant said, 'Paul Schneider, born 29 August 1897, died today at 10.40 a.m. If transport of the body at the family's expense is required, a request must be made within twenty-four hours ... otherwise the body will be cremated.'

Gretel arranged for the body to be brought home. Three days after his murder, Paul's remains were buried in the churchyard at Dickenschied. In less than two months Hitler's plan to begin the nightmare of the Second World War would take effect.

Gretel and the six children survived the horror of that war.[21] She lived as a widow until her death on 27 December 2002, twelve days before her ninety-ninth birthday. She lived to see all her children grow up, and her husband become respected as a martyr by the Evangelical Church of the Rhineland. There is even a Pastor Paul Schneider Association, founded at Weimar in 1997, dedicated to keeping his memory alive. Visitors to his cell in the bunker at Buchenwald can now see his photograph, a plaque in honour of his sacrifice and the words of a biblical text selected by his widow: 'We are ... Christ's ambassadors, as though God were making his appeal through us. We implore you on Christ's behalf: Be reconciled to God' (2 Corinthians 5:20).

More information on Paul Schneider

Once the Second World War was over, Schneider's widow published his story in German (1953). E. H. Robertson translated it into English. The book was published by SCM in 1956 as *The Pastor of Buchenwald.*

Occasional articles appeared in the years that followed. Pastor Victor Budgen wrote for *Evangelical Times* and *Reformation Today* (issue 54 March/April 1980).

All previous work was superseded in 1997 when Claude R. Foster, Jr., a history professor, wrote *Paul Schneider: The Buchenwald Apostle.* This definitive sourcebook runs to 901 pages and contains a great deal of new information, much of it derived from Gretel Schneider. West Chester University Press publishes it. Requests for copies of Dr Foster's large book should be sent to S.S.I. Bookstore, West Chester University, West Chester, PA 19383, USA. A German translation is available.

A DVD lasting twenty minutes called 'You mass murderers—I accuse you' has been produced by the Evangelical Church of the Rhineland. It can be ordered via the Pastor Paul Schneider Association, whose website is:

www.angelfire.com/pa5/paulschneider

This contains details of membership and other relevant information. The goals of the association are:

To preserve the knowledge of Paul Schneider's faithful witness in a day of moral ambiguity.

To encourage other Christians to take a stand, when necessary, for faith and conscience.

To influence our daily thought as to how a Christian life can be lived.

3

William Dobbie

Defender of Malta

Perceptively, Churchill wrote of William Dobbie that he was 'a Governor of outstanding character who inspired all ranks and classes, military and civil, with his determination; a Cromwellian figure at the key point ... fighting with his Bible in one hand and his sword in the other'.

Lt.-Gen. Sir William Dobbie, GCMG, KCB, DSO

3

William Dobbie

'Defend Malta at all costs.' This was no easy order for any British commanding officer in early 1940. It filled General William Dobbie's mind as his plane landed on the island in the early hours of Sunday, 28 April. The new governor and commander-in-chief was sixty, recently retired with forty years' service behind him. He was about to face the severest challenge of his life.

Within weeks of his arrival, Hitler became master of Western Europe. When his fascist ally, Mussolini, dictator of Italy, joined him in making war on Britain, they formed a genuine axis of evil.

Malta is a little island in the Mediterranean Sea, seventeen miles long and nine miles at its widest. It is like an unsinkable 'aircraft carrier' anchored sixty miles away from Italian territory. From it the British had the potential to ruin the enemy's supply route and its 'Grand Plan', which was to be an attempt to seize North Africa as a hopeful prelude to pushing east through Egypt to southern Russia and its oil. It was all part of the dream of worldwide conquest.

Two years later, after furious fighting that involved an average of three immense air raids a day, Malta remained bloody but unbowed, in spite of literally being 'the most bombed place on the earth'.

One officer who watched Dobbie while bombs were falling all around him remarked, 'He paid no more attention to them than to rain.'[1]

Another man who served alongside him later made a BBC broadcast in which he described him as 'a big man—big physically, big professionally, and big morally'.[2]

Francis Gerard also knew him at first hand during the siege. In his book *Malta Magnificent*, he comments on Dobbie's 'complete fearlessness'[3] amidst the crash and choking dust of the bombs.

Perceptively, Churchill wrote of William Dobbie that he was 'a Governor of outstanding character who inspired all ranks and classes, military and civil, with his determination; a Cromwellian figure at the key point ... fighting with his Bible in one hand and his sword in the other.'

Dobbie found his way into the history books for leading the British response to Italian and German aggression on Malta, but the rest of his career has largely been overlooked.

Before William was born in India in 1879, the Dobbie family had long been committed Christians. His father was in the Indian Civil Service and other relatives served in the army. The Christian faith would be a marked feature of the life of William Dobbie. As a Christian he 'practised the presence of God'. No matter what the circumstances, he prayed. His writings are filled with references to his faith and the nearness of God.

He had a conversion experience while at Charterhouse School. On the first Sunday in November 1893, when he was fourteen, he felt 'that things were not right between God and me and that I was unfit to stand in his sight'. Dobbie felt his unworthiness when confronted by the holiness of God. This sense of inadequacy became a spiritual burden. Later, summing up his feelings, he recorded: 'My need of a Saviour was brought home to me.'

William Dobbie wrote that '… Jesus Christ, the Son of God, came into this world for the express purpose of giving his life so that he might bear, and pay the penalty of my sin so that I might go free. That night I accepted the Lord Jesus as my Saviour, my Companion, and my God—just by myself—there was nobody else in the room. That was the turning point of my life. The past, bad though it was in God's sight, was blotted out; Christ's presence and help were promised for the present, and the future was assured. I thank God more than I can say for that wonderful event in November 1893.'[4]

What Dobbie describes is a typical sudden evangelical conversion. Saul on the Damascus road is a biblical example of this. Dobbie did not doubt that an authentic personal relationship with God had been formed. There were no second thoughts. He was baptized as a believer and attached himself to what would now be called an Open Brethren evangelical church.

He took the usual Christian view that there is meaning to life as a whole and therefore that God must have a plan for his life. Charterhouse School had entered him for the examination to enter the Royal Military Academy, Woolwich. He passed. Though there was a pacifist tradition in his church, he accepted the open door into the academy as God's plan that he should become a soldier.

It was 1897. Dobbie was six feet three inches (1.90 metres) tall, solidly built, athletic and clever. Two years later he was commissioned as a second lieutenant in the Royal Engineers. He was a sapper, a military engineer.

His first public military duty was to be part of the guard at Queen Victoria's funeral in 1901. Smart in full-dress scarlet uniform, he stood by the park railings at Piccadilly. Soon afterwards he was plunged into the middle of the Boer War. Interestingly, he later took the view that this was an unjust war.

In 1904, again in full-dress uniform, he married Sybil. They had three children, one of whom was subsequently killed fighting the Nazis in Italy in 1944.

After various overseas postings, he decided to take the entrance examinations for the British Army's Staff College at Camberley. He was top of the fifty successful men in 1911. His graduation coincided with the outbreak of World War I in 1914.

Dobbie endured the horrors of that war, starting as a captain and ending as a lieutenant colonel. When the British regulars came up against the Germans at Mons in 1914, it was numbers that overwhelmed them, not greater bravery or skill. Dobbie played a full part in the retreat from Mons. In 1915 shrapnel smashed the binoculars round his neck. On Christmas Day that year he walked along seventeen miles of British trenches in eight and a half hours with the aim of lifting the morale of the British troops.

He did not talk much about his work and what he had suffered. People often asked him what he did in the war. The usual laconic answer was: 'I ended it.' By that he meant that he was the officer on duty at British General Headquarters when news of the armistice was received. Dobbie dictated a telegram intended for every British soldier:

> Hostilities will cease at 11.00 hours today. Troops will stand fast at the line reached at that hour. There will be no fraternization with the enemy.
> Signed: W. G. S. Dobbie. Lieut. Colonel, General Staff.
> 11 November 1918.[5]

When personal letters to his wife became available, they showed in more detail how he reacted when surrounded by death and destruction on a vast scale. By nature, she was prone to worry. In contrast, he always looked on the bright side of life. Frequently he tells her after a battle: 'Our men were absolutely magnificent.'

He took the same view of the enemy soldiers: 'The Germans opposite us are a fine lot and fought magnificently.' Sybil had doubts that he would survive the war, given the high casualty rate. Nor was she convinced that victory was possible. Dobbie tried to alter her perceptions. One letter gives her spiritual advice: 'Please don't try and bear the burden of things when the Lord wants to bear the burden for you.' Nobody who has any idea of the extent of the slaughter in the 1914–1918 war would have disagreed with Dobbie's sentiment when he wrote, 'Please God, this fighting will shorten the war.'[6]

Some men blamed God for the war; Dobbie blamed the sin embedded in the heart of every man. Some lost whatever 'faith' they had; by contrast, Dobbie emerged from the carnage and misery as a Christian soldier who had grown closer to, and more dependent on, God. There were other soldiers like him with strong views about being a Christian believer in the midst of killing and terror. Brave chaplains and stretcher-bearers are examples, in addition to the men who did the fighting and dying. He mentions joining the Soldiers' Christian Association (now the Soldiers' and Airmen's Scripture Readers' Association or SASRA). This included men of all ranks who met together to encourage one another. Sybil was told that the SCA 'have got a large room at Étaples where they hold meetings nightly with hundreds present'.[7] His letters always reveal a man who did not just ask for God's help; he genuinely experienced God's nearness on a daily basis.

One incident in March 1918 made a big impression on him. Because Russia had made peace as a result of the Bolshevik Revolution of 1917, the German army was no longer fighting in the east. So all its resources could be aimed solely at the British and French in the west. At the time Dobbie was serving on the staff of the British commander-in-chief, Douglas Haig. The German army was on the verge of pushing the French and British armies apart.

At the end of March it became necessary to move a particular British division from the north to prevent a total breakthrough. If the Germans succeeded they would win the war. Dobbie knew all this. He telephoned for railway carriages to transport the men of the division immediately. The officer in charge of the rail links replied that it was impossible. No amount of argument or using higher rank worked. Dobbie records that he prayed, 'Lord, I have come to the end of my tether. It seems necessary to have that division if we are not to lose the war. Please help.'[8]

Shortly afterwards the telephone rang. The rolling stock had unexpectedly become available. The division plugged the hole the Germans were punching in the defensive line.

In his book *A Very Present Help* Dobbie admits that this story raises many problems. For instance, it appears to suggest that God takes sides. It could have been a coincidence that railway vehicles became available when they did. What if a German was praying the opposite? But, whatever happened, he continued, 'I had no doubt in my mind that God intervened.'[9] After all, he reasoned, the Bible is filled with stories of answered prayer. Furthermore, in Bible stories about war, God is often said to take sides.

On 4 August 1918 the British called an official day of prayer that was more widely observed than had been expected. British troops assembled near Amiens for a huge counter-attack. Surprise would save lives on both sides. It was physically impossible to conceal so many units. But suddenly the weather prevented German aircraft from flying over and seeing what was going on. Four days after the day of prayer the Battle of Amiens began a hundred days of victories that led to the final German defeat. General Ludendorff, the German chief of staff, called this moment 'the black day of the German army'.[10]

Interestingly, the next national day of prayer was held on 26 May 1940, though the decision pre-dated that Sunday. Dobbie's son was one of the helpless British soldiers hoping to be brought home from Dunkirk. In his desperation at the possible capture of the British army, King George VI called for a national day of prayer. Churchill's government supported him. Shortly after this, the English Channel went calm, so allowing boats an easy crossing to save the men stranded on Dunkirk's beaches. Even more remarkably, Hitler stopped his tank units from attacking. Historians still argue why he did it. The fact remains that this decision saved the army. Almost all the men were rescued. Churchill called it 'a great deliverance'.

William Dobbie contributed his piece to the mosaic of victory. As a result of his work in the First World War he was awarded the Distinguished Service Order (DSO). Six times the big, blonde Dobbie was 'mentioned in dispatches' for 'gallant and distinguished services on the battlefield'. Also, the French gave him military honours, the Croix de Guerre and the Légion d'Honneur. So did the Belgians.

In 1929 Dobbie was in charge of operations during the Palestine Emergency. The League of Nations, formed after the First World War, gave Britain the task, or mandate, to rule Palestine. Tensions between Jews and Arabs emerged almost immediately.

Based at Jerusalem, Dobbie had too few British troops available to keep the peace. The town of Gaza was in the path of several thousand armed Bedouin known to be intent on murder and looting. A British mission hospital was a target for these men, who were inflamed by propaganda and hate. Dobbie wrote, 'In my need I asked for God's special help and intervention. I knelt down and told him that I was at the end of my resources.'[11] For a while the Arabs pushed on, hiding in caves and gullies from British aircraft. Suddenly, 'For no reason I was able to ascertain, they changed direction at right angles, and instead of completing the short distance to Gaza, they spent the night in open country, a long way from anything that mattered.'[12]

Early the next morning HMS *Courageous* arrived at Jaffa from

Malta carrying a battalion of soldiers. Trains rushed the troops to
Gaza. Dobbie asked his political officers to find out why the Bedouin
had changed direction. No rational explanation was ever discovered.
For his part, Dobbie believed it was an answer to prayer. Without
having resorted to martial law, he handed over a pacified Palestine to
the new commander-in-chief, Air Vice-Marshal Dowding.

The British government was impressed, and commended
Dobbie's handling of the 1929 Palestine Emergency.

The Bible calls the place where Christ was crucified 'the place
of the skull'. Dobbie's office in Jerusalem looked out onto a hill
often called 'Gordon's Calvary'. Back in 1883, General Gordon
had noticed that this hill had the shape and appearance of a skull.

A Bible Society wished to distribute New Testaments to the
brigade of British troops under Dobbie's command. He agreed,
and in the office gazing at the hill looking like a skull, he wrote a
statement to go with each New Testament. It reads:

> You are stationed at the place where the central event
> in human history occurred—namely the crucifixion of the
> Son of God. You may see the place where this happened and
> you may read the details in this book. As you do this, you
> cannot help being interested, but your interest will change
> into something far deeper when you realize that the event
> concerns you personally. It was for your sake that the Son
> of God died on the cross here. The realization of this fact
> cannot but produce a radical change in one's life—and the
> study of this book will, under God's guidance, help you to
> such a realization.
>
> Signed: W. G. S. Dobbie   Jerusalem
> Brigadier   10 October 1929[13]

His remaining tours of duty involved a few years as officer
commanding the School of Military Engineering at Chatham.

This was one of the highest specialist sapper appointments. After that he spent 1935 to 1939 in command of the fortress of Singapore. Here he realized that the potential enemy, the Japanese, could easily come in by the 'back door'. Funds for the defence of Singapore from an enemy invasion from the north were requested and refused. His attitude to the defence of Singapore was clear in his response when General Armitage told him, 'You might be the one to hand over Singapore to the Japanese.' Dobbie's reply was: 'We'll eat rats first.'[14] Tragically, in 1941 the fortress fell in exactly the way he had foreseen.

When World War II started he was totally frustrated at being unable to do anything to help his beleaguered country. Then came the appointment to Malta.

The fighting power of Malta was quickly assessed. He commanded about 5,000 troops. At first there were only sixteen old anti-aircraft guns on the island. Four old Gladiator biplane fighters were discovered in overlooked crates. Three were assembled. They were nicknamed 'Faith', 'Hope' and 'Charity'. For a time they provided the total air defence of Malta. Amazingly, one still survives in a museum on Malta.

Britain herself was under threat of invasion by Hitler in 1940. No reinforcements from home could be expected. The nearest British bases were Gibraltar, almost 1,000 miles west, and Alexandria, nearly 1,000 miles east. Instead, the most senior British army officer, Sir Edmund Ironside, sent a telegram from London. It said, 'Deuteronomy chapter three verse twenty two.'[15] Dobbie had a look at this verse in the Bible. It says, 'Do not be afraid of them; for the LORD your God himself will fight for you.'

Although Malta's future looked very uncertain, Dobbie the optimist always believed that Britain would win the war. He did not know how. Nor did Churchill.

When France was defeated by Germany in 1940, Dobbie addressed the Maltese people: 'The decision of the British

government to fight on until our enemies are defeated will have
been heard with the greatest satisfaction by all the garrison of
Malta. It may be that hard times lie ahead of us, but however
hard they may be, I know that our courage and determination will
not falter. With God's help we will maintain the security of this
fortress. I therefore call upon all of us to seek God's help, and then,
in reliance on him, to do our duty unflinchingly.'[16]

Italy's declaration of war on Britain came on 10 June 1940.
The first air raid on Malta followed at 06.00 the next morning.
Dobbie's broadcast to the Maltese people included these words:
'May God help us each one to do our duty unstintingly.'[17]

270,000 Maltese heard what he said. The joke among them was
that the people were more Catholic than the pope. Yet both the
population and their religious leaders liked and respected their
decidedly Protestant governor. As a consequence, he gained and
kept the full confidence of the Maltese people. This is a credit to
him.

His straightforward honesty impressed them. He could be seen
among crowds of hungry children, in the deep rock tunnels of the
island, in the sun-baked streets of the towns, indeed anywhere
there was need or trouble. He never resorted to a shelter. The raids
did not cause him to cancel an activity. His courage was infectious.

Military historians today are astonished that Mussolini and
Hitler failed to invade Malta, instead of trying to bomb it into
submission. Both of the dictators had pre-arranged plans, but they
were never implemented. Dobbie put it down to God's restraining
hand. Whatever explanation is given, it is certain that failure
to capture Malta resulted in the island being used by British
submarines, ships and planes that sank numerous ships carrying
supplies to enemy armies in North Africa. Rommel, the German
commander, attributed much of the cause of his ultimate defeat
in the battles for North Africa to the military performance of the
fortress of Malta.

In his book *A Very Present Help* Dobbie records some incidents that made a big impression on him. One related to a convoy of supplies that reached Malta in January 1941. Among the convoy's escort ships was a new aircraft carrier, HMS *Illustrious*. This ship limped into Malta already badly damaged by bombs. Once in the dockyard, the German Luftwaffe decided to make sure she would never leave Malta. They scored many hits. The prospects for saving *Illustrious* looked small. After a while, the dockyard authorities told Dobbie that *if there were no further damage* she could go to sea in four days' time. Only Dobbie knew what the dockyard had indicated. He prayed to God about it. He recorded: 'The next day came. The attacks were renewed, but the Germans changed their tactics and bombed from a much greater height than before. They missed the ship—and no further damage was done. The same thing was experienced on the three following days; and, eventually, on the fourth day, after sunset, I saw the great ship head for Alexandria, which she safely reached.'[18]

On another occasion the cruiser HMS *Penelope* had to enter dry dock in Malta for repairs. The enemy planes found her, like a sitting duck, helpless to avoid their bombs. *Penelope* was hit so often that her crew called her 'HMS Pepper Pot', full of holes on top! The strange thing was that no vital damage was done. Necessary repairs were completed. Looking very much like a porcupine because of the large number of wooden plugs sticking out of her, she left Malta and fought her way to Gibraltar. On her arrival there was a service of thanksgiving on deck. Dobbie wrote, 'The whole thing was a miracle.'[19]

In April 1942, while Dobbie was still governor, King George VI awarded Malta the George Cross. This was the first of only two occasions in British history that an entire community has been honoured for valour. (The other was the Royal Ulster Constabulary in the twenty-first century.)

As the 2,300th air raid hit Malta on 7 May 1942, Dobbie

was taken to Britain on the flying boat that brought in the next governor, Lord Gort. Four days later Dobbie was in hospital with a ruptured appendix. He was sixty-two.

Speaking at Malta's Council of Government, Gort summed up the story: 'Malta owes much to Sir William Dobbie. It was he who organized this fortress for war. It was his foresight that produced the shelters. It was under his administration that the foundations were laid of the great civil organization which was destined to carry the siege through to a successful conclusion.'[20]

Dobbie died aged eighty-five on 3 October 1964. He summed up the testimony of his life in these words: 'Vital and uninterrupted contact with our Heavenly Father is the most wonderful thing in the world.'

His faith in Christ was preserved through war and danger, through fame and success, through bereavement and old age. That contact with God, rooted in Scripture, was never broken.

More information on William Dobbie

Several short accounts of the life of William Dobbie have appeared. The January/February 1965 issue of *Practical Christianity* (the magazine for officers in the three services), carried articles of remembrance. A good obituary appears in *The Evangelical Library Bulletin* Spring 1965 issue. Brigadier W. I. C. Dobbie wrote an excellent summary of his life in the December 1999 issue of *Evangelical Times*.

Brigadier Dobbie possesses one copy of a privately printed biography by William Dobbie's daughter, Sybil. The title is *Faith and Fortitude*. Brigadier Dobbie very kindly lent it to me, and I have leaned on it heavily. Not even the Evangelical Library appears to own a copy.

William Dobbie's own writings, *Active Service with Christ* and *A Very Present Help*, should be read by anyone interested in his faith and life.

The Internet displays a short film clip of Dobbie arriving back in England after serving in Malta. It can be seen at

www.britishpathe.com/video/dobbie-of-malta-comes-home

4

Johanna-Ruth Dobschiner

Holocaust survivor

The doorbell rang, and did not stop ringing, until the door was opened. Hansie heard heavy footsteps on the stairs. A voice shouted, 'Hurry up. We haven't got all night.' Her father and mother were forced out and pushed into a waiting army lorry. Hansie lay frozen with terror in her bed ...

Johanna-Ruth Dobschiner

4

Johanna-Ruth Dobschiner[1]

Moving quickly, fourteen-year-old Johanna-Ruth Dobschiner, known as Hansie to family and friends, drew back the curtains of her bedroom window.

Aroused early by the unexpected noise of aircraft and gunfire over Amsterdam, she saw that the street outside was full of neighbours. Most of them were pointing upwards and looking agitated. It was very early on Friday morning, 10 May 1940. When Hansie looked up she was astounded to see the sky full of parachute troops. Not many hours later, she saw the terrifying sight of grey-uniformed German troops in her own street. A horrendous time had begun.

The world soon learned that at 04.30 on that morning of the 10th May Hitler had attacked a genuinely neutral country without declaring war. The Dutch had taken no part in the First World War. At the end of it they had even provided a home for life for Wilhelm, the defeated German Kaiser. Hitler had only one reason for unleashing his vast army against the unsuspecting Dutch: parts of their territory offered easy routes for him to deliver attacks on the British and French. The peace-loving Dutch, who had not fought a war since 1830, were beaten into submission within five days. The extremely brutal occupation of their country lasted for five years.

What happened next was particularly frightening to Hansie's family. Their original home had been in Berlin. Hansie and her two older brothers, Werner and Manfred, had been born there. Seeing the writing on the wall, the Dutch consul advised them to flee from the rising tide of Nazi anti-Jewish prejudice and physical assaults. Hansie was only nine and looking forward to living in the safety of Holland. That was in 1935. When the German troops landed on them literally 'out of the blue', the dreaded enemy they had left behind had caught up with them. There had been exactly five years free from menace and terror.

Things quickly became worse in Holland. The Dutch queen, Wilhelmina, warned her people that she might be kidnapped and used as a hostage. Reluctantly she escaped to England on a British destroyer. The rest of the population was trapped. Within days the new German government started issuing laws. The majority of them were directed against the Jewish people, though any Dutch citizen who resisted the illegal occupation could also be in trouble. There was no way of evading the power of the invaders.

New regulations demanded that Jews hand over personal possessions such as cars, bicycles and radios. Notices appeared outside shops, hotels, theatres and cinemas announcing: 'Forbidden to Jews.' They were not allowed to use public transport. A miserable Hansie was forced to leave her integrated school and attend an all-Jewish school. Early in 1941 a new law stipulated that all Jews had to purchase bright yellow stars five inches (twelve and a half centimetres) wide with the word 'JEW' in capital letters written on them. The stars had to be stitched on all clothing worn outdoors. Anyone who did not wear the star was punished severely, but in the first stage of the occupation it was not a matter of life and death.

On 21 February 1941 anti-Semitism did become a life-and-death issue. Hansie's two brothers were among many thousands of male Jews randomly rounded up off the streets and sent to concentration camps. Hansie insisted for the rest of her life that her mother's hair went white overnight. As feared, her two brothers were never seen again. Her parents eventually received some ashes.

Hansie's ambition was to be a nurse, but for the time being she had to be content with helping a dressmaker. As more and more Jewish people went to the 'land of no return', as she put it, fear gripped her and her thoughts became increasingly fixed on the Jewish Hospital. She had the idea that she would be safe as a patient in the hospital. A friendly nursing sister arranged for the unnecessary removal of her appendix. Hansie judged that her appendix was worth two weeks of peace of mind and safety.

In the autumn of 1942 she felt genuinely ill and a doctor diagnosed scarlet fever. Rules required a sign to be put up at the door of the house: 'Danger. No entry. Scarlet fever.' Evidently the Nazis did not like infectious illness. The disease brought six weeks of welcome security. As she lay in bed, her very devout orthodox Jewish parents celebrated the Feast of Hanukkah. This comes in December at about the same time as Christmas.

Confined to bed in an upstairs room, and on her own for much of the time, Hansie thought about recent events. She definitely believed in the Jewish religion and its observances. She was Jewish, and did not want to be anything else. But something was missing from this seventeen-year-old's life. She analysed her religion and that of her parents. It was strict in outward observance of the festivals, yet God seemed distant. God was not part of their everyday lives even though they were so religious. It shook her deeply to think that God was not treated as a present reality. Orthodox Judaism offered festivals, such as Hanukkah, to remember the actions of God in the history of the Hebrew people. She started asking herself whether she could know God personally *now*. If God was real, could he be contacted? Why did her religion make him seem so remote?

During December 1942 she went through an experience that she described like this: 'I became "God-conscious" for the first time in my life ... This remote person, the Almighty God, allowed me a glimpse of Himself ... I now knew that God not only was, but *is* ... Three words now stood rock-like in my life: "GOD ... WITH ... US." I knew myself close to God that evening.'

To share this message of comfort and assurance, she wrote the three words on three pieces of paper, and pinned them to the wall above her bed. The intention was good. If the family trusted in the truth of the words, they would find encouragement. That was how she reasoned.

However, when she shared this 'moment of revelation' about the nearness of God with her parents, she was interrupted by her father's comment: 'Don't talk such utter rubbish.' Plainly the notion that God could be known as a daily reality was not for a devout orthodox Jew. Though she most certainly had not become a Christian, the strange spiritual experience of the nearness of God sustained her through the dreadful events of the next two years.

By February 1943 the scarlet fever was gone. The smell of Dettol antiseptic dispersed, and the notice warning about infectious disease had to come down. The Dobschiner family returned to 'normal'. All of them felt that the sword of Damocles was hanging over them by a very thin thread.

At 22.00 on 9 April 1943 came the bitterest blow of all. The cat-and-mouse existence ended. The doorbell rang, and did not stop ringing, until the door was opened. Hansie heard heavy footsteps on the stairs. A voice shouted, 'Hurry up. We haven't got all night.' Her father and mother were forced out and pushed into a waiting army lorry. Hansie lay frozen with terror in her bed, which was hidden by a partition in the room. To her amazement the soldiers did not see her. The door banged and she was totally alone in a silent house.

Her brain worked at top speed. At first she remained motionless, mostly out of fear. Then she realized the danger she was in. Looters, who always seemed to know when a family had been arrested, might come before curfew ended. Acting quickly, she dressed, put a few essentials in a little black case and walked out as soon as 06.00 came. She dare not return. As she walked away, dazed and in a state of shock, she glanced back. It had been such a lovely flat with a good view of the canal and its barges.

She reported for duty at the Jewish day nursery where she worked. All she had to say was: 'They came last night … the whole family.' The others understood without further explanation. On a dreary April morning she watched the ghastly scene as dozens of army lorries lined up ready to receive the pathetic lines of helpless people. Then she saw her mother and father. She wanted to wave to them, but did not dare. If a soldier saw the movement of a curtain and a wave, he might simply point at the window. Other soldiers would burst into the building and take her to join the victims who had already been arrested. It was essential to resist the temptation to wave. Lorries' engines revved, and then they were all gone. She would never see her parents again. The awful deed, a living burial, was done.

Hansie's parents were among over 100,000 Dutch Jews murdered during the five years of Nazi occupation. The most well-known was teenager Anne Frank. The diary she kept before she was betrayed was published after her death.

On Sunday, 20 June 1943, Hansie was seized from the house where she was lodging. Soldiers were everywhere, ordering people into waiting army lorries. Some Dutch Nazi black-shirt traitors were on hand to help with 'language problems'. Amazed at her own composure, Hansie said to her escorts in German, 'Can I do anything to help?' In her own mind she thought that she could look after some crying children. The offer was accepted. She could mind lost children.

When they reached the railway station in Amsterdam, the children were reunited with their parents. The scene on the station was one of confusion. The adult victims stood around, just accepting what was happening to them. German soldiers ordered a goods train to be filled up. Fifty prisoners about to make the journey to death were to go in every cattle truck. The Jews were packed in like animals. There were no seats and no sanitation.

Before long it was Hansie's turn to climb into a cattle truck. She helped to lift a pram aboard. The family's baby was crying. The child was covered with red spots. In a desperate attempt to escape, the 'nurse' used her fluency in German. Through the bars she cried out loudly, 'Attention. Attention. Infectious disease. Open the door at once. Highly infectious family in this wagon. Hurry! Hurry!'

To her astonishment, nearby soldiers opened the door. Boldly, she ordered them to keep their distance. An officer told her that as a nurse she was in charge of the family! They were to go to the station waiting room. With the help of a friendly Dutch doctor, the resourceful seventeen-year-old continued the pretence that what were probably only heat spots were in fact the symptoms of scarlet fever. Trains came and went, clearing the station of its human misery. Finally, Dr van Ebo arranged for the family and a few others to be loaded into an ambulance. Still wearing her yellow star, Hansie climbed in with the family. The ambulance headed for the hospital. In this way, she escaped death once again. Another nightmare was over—for the time being.

Without informing Hansie, Dr van Ebo had told the hospital matron what his young helper had done on Amsterdam railway station. As a result, the Jewish City Hospital employed Hansie Dobschiner as a nurse, even though she was unqualified. All the time she was there, she wondered how safe she really was. When would she be taken away to a concentration camp? It seemed as though the answer came on 5 July 1943.

Officers from the Gestapo came to the hospital, took over the loudspeaker system, and read out the names of everybody who had been employed there for less than three months. 'H. Dobschiner' was one person named. Still in uniform, she was bundled into a lorry. They went through familiar streets to a waiting train.

Hansie climbed into a compartment. Before they moved off, a lady, also on the journey to oblivion, asked Hansie on which ward she had worked. 'Infectious diseases,' was the reply. Did they not have enough trouble without catching infectious illness from her? A chorus of voices pleaded with her: 'Please go; please leave us.' To Hansie it seemed ironic to be concerned about any sort of infection in such a situation.

She broke all the rules and stepped out on to the platform. At once a soldier approached. Ignoring the pointing rifle, she spoke in her Berlin accent: 'It's no use; they won't have me in the train because I worked in the isolation unit for infectious diseases. I think I had better go back to the hospital. Have you any transport please?'

The soldier lowered his gun and turned to another soldier: 'Are you going back to the city? Drop this nurse at the hospital, will you? Thanks.'

It worked! Hansie was the only person to return to the hospital that day. All the others went to death camps.

The matron in charge of the Jewish Hospital assigned Hansie to district nursing. Her orders were to care for a woman with pneumonia called Mrs Sim. One day Mr Sim returned from work very early. Out of breath, he gasped, 'They are doing your hospital. It's dreadful.' Sure enough, the hospital was emptied. All doctors, nurses and patients were sent to their deaths. Hansie was saved only because she was off the premises. This inhuman deed occurred on 13 August 1943.

Hansie was now a couple of weeks away from her eighteenth birthday. However, the will to live was ebbing out of her. She became inwardly convinced that her turn to be rounded up was now inevitable. Were all these attempts to escape worthwhile? She decided to end the mental torture by giving herself up. She even chose a date to surrender: 6 September. Hearing of her decision, a friend, Lena, physically restrained her from walking into captivity. 'You selfish, stupid, childish idiot,' her friend yelled. 'Get back at once and stop your nonsense.'

Having been restrained from 'committing deliberate suicide', as Lena described it, consider Hansie's surprise when on the following day some anti-Nazi Dutch people offered her the opportunity to go 'underground'. This meant that there was the possibility of going into long-term hiding somewhere. Another Jewish girl had been the first choice, but was in bed with influenza. Because the next day was the deadline, Hansie was selected as a substitute.

8 September 1943 was the great day. The instructions were simple, and given to protect everyone involved. They were communicated by Jan, a hall porter who had worked in the hospital. She must memorize, not write down, an address in Amsterdam East. At the corner of that street she was to sneeze and take a handkerchief out of the right-hand pocket of her coat. As directed, she went to the house. Reaching the address, she knocked at the door and walked into the house—and into a new way of life.

A tall slim man greeted her. She had to take him on trust since she had no idea who he was. It might well have been a trap. Instead the man told her to call herself Francisca Dobber from then on. He cut off her yellow star. She changed out of her nurse's uniform. The man said that she could call him 'Domie'. Together they took a train to the north of Holland, where he hid her in his house along with five other young people.

In Holland Christian ministers are usually called 'Dominie'. Domie was in fact Bastian Johan Ader, an evangelical minister of the Dutch Reformed Church. Aged thirty-three when he met Hansie, he was a key figure in the Dutch resistance to the Nazi occupation. Bastian Ader not only sheltered Jews; he protected airmen who had been shot down and arranged for them to be smuggled back to England. As well as these activities, he kept up a Reformed biblical ministry near Groningen in the north of Holland. No wonder that one of Hansie's first impressions of him was that he seemed tired. He is one of the world's little-known great men.

In the safety of Bastian Ader's home in the countryside at Nieuw-Beerta, Hansie was away from the world of soldiers, arrests, curfews and raids. Ader's wife, Jo, had one young son and another on the way, so Hansie helped around the house. It turned out to be tense and lonely waiting for liberation as the Allied armies slowly pushed the Germans back. News of Allied progress after D-Day, 6 June 1944, came from the BBC in London on an illegal radio located in the attic of the church house.

Hansie kept up her Jewish religion as much as the solitude allowed. Hundreds of books lined the walls of every room in Domie's home. One day in early 1944, as she was looking at the titles, she found an illustrated Children's Bible. She decided to read it. Chores were done, and time passed so slowly that boredom was a problem. Most of the stories it contained were familiar to a religious Jew, such as those about Moses and the prophets. Then for the very first time she read the story of Jesus Christ. It was puzzling. Why had she never been told before about this Jewish prophet? The more she read, the more she admired Jesus. She commented, 'As the weeks and months passed by, his life became part of mine. I enjoyed the company of my Bible and my new-found prophet and hero, Jesus.'

One day she unearthed a Bible in Dutch. After reading the Old Testament, there was a blank page before a new title page. On that title page was printed: 'The New Testament of our Lord and Saviour Jesus Christ'. Following this were four books about Jesus called 'Gospels'—Matthew, Mark, Luke and John. She read the four short books, and some of the following books, with growing interest. It became easy to understand why these Christians, such as Domie, or 'Uncle Bas' as she now called him, acted as they did.

One Sunday morning in February 1944, she asked if she could join the others in a secret position from which she could observe the church service. It was the first Christian message from the Bible that she had ever heard. Domie preached from John chapter 13. Hansie sensed his sincerity. The power of the sermon reached her heart. The whole story of the life, death and resurrection of Jesus, and its implications for her, became clear.

During one evening in April 1944, Domie informed the group that he must go into hiding because the Nazis were determined to arrest him. They would have to move quickly before his house and church were raided. As they all dispersed Hansie asked Domie's wife for permission to take the Dutch Bible with her. She consented—and seemed not the least bit surprised.

Moved from one safe house to another, Hansie was helpless. Her future, if she had one, was in the hands of Domie and his friends. She knew that these ordinary Dutch people were freely accepting a fearful risk. They could be shot for hiding her. Days and weeks dragged by. More and more her thoughts turned to the Bible.

She wrote, '[God] was explained and portrayed so clearly by … Jesus Christ, that I almost felt that I knew Him—that I could depend on him—that I could take Him at His word and live according to His advice. It only worried me when this Jesus Christ made definite claims regarding his purpose on earth or his authority; or proclaimed His ... divinity and the part He played in our approach to the Almighty Creator of the Universe. Some of His ... words would come to me:

"No one cometh unto the Father, but by me."

"I am the way, the truth, and the life."

"Come unto me ... and I will give you rest."

"All power is given to me in heaven and in earth."

"I am come that they might have life." '

Then she recorded: 'Unconsciously, He had stolen His way into my life, and I could no more think of God the Father without visualizing Jesus Christ. Slowly but surely, God became a reality ... As day succeeded day [Christ drew] me closer and closer to his heart ... What reason did we have to disbelieve this Jesus, when He claimed that He was that promised Messiah who would die for our sins and rise again to be the first of those to conquer death? ... A vital truth surged through my very being ... He's alive! ... It was [Jesus] who had been busy with me all these months. His vast almighty and penetrating Holy Spirit had pierced my iron curtain of reasoning.'

On Easter Monday 1944, Hansie was sharing the attic of a safe house in the south of Holland with Sister Moony. They had known each other in the Jewish Hospital in Amsterdam. Neither had realized the other was still alive. Back in the period when she had worked in the hospital, Hansie had looked up to the sister with awe and dread because she was such a bossy person. However, in the attic they were just two equal human beings. A plaque above the attic door proclaimed a verse from the Old Testament which says, 'Man looks at the outward appearance, but the LORD looks at the heart' (1 Samuel 16:7).

Hansie's search for a relationship with a personal God came to an end that Easter Monday. Once chores were done, all her waking hours were taken up with the study of the little black Bible in Dutch. She was oblivious to the once-domineering presence of Sister Moony. As she read, God became more and more real. Matters came to a conclusion with an act of faith and commitment. Hansie was peeling potatoes. She laid down the knife, rose from the stool, and walked to a spot among the attic beams in a little corner of the roof. 'I slowly knelt down, clasped my hands in absolute surrender and closed my eyes to all around. "Rabboni Joshua Hamoschiach" ("Master Jesus Christ"). It was all I could whisper. Deep thankfulness and love to Almighty God for his inexplicable revelation and gift flooded my entire being. God cared. He cared after all!'

By the end of Easter Monday 1944, even though she had been a Christian for only hours, Sister Moony asked her why she seemed so happy. 'My inward happiness had spilled over and made her wonder,' she thought.

During the next few weeks, she eagerly read all she could from both Old and New Testaments. She felt as though she had entered a different world, one with a life that was endless. She was totally secure spiritually because she was in the hands of her majestic Creator, and his appointed prophesied Saviour.

In later years the writer spent hours discussing Hansie's wartime experiences with her. She explained, among other things, how she found these words of Jesus in Matthew's Gospel: 'Do not be afraid of those who kill the body but cannot kill the soul. Rather, be afraid of the one who can destroy both soul and body in hell' (Matthew 10:28). That was strong language, she thought. Even if she were arrested now, *her* Master would look after her, even if she had to die.

The spiritual experience that happened in moments lasted a lifetime. By faith she came to know the risen Christ. Domie and his wife were good examples, but no human being gave her new life. Christ did that directly. No human mediators were involved. It was a living faith in the living God who became real to her as she read the pages of Scripture. She never repudiated her Jewish background, but she was Christ's disciple from that Easter Monday in 1944 for as long as she lived.

She described her experience like this: 'Never before did I have such close fellowship with Christ, the irresistible Christ, whose existence some people deny.' When the air-raid sirens sounded and people ran for shelter, she wrote, 'Christ stayed with me. His Holy Spirit, able to be everywhere at the same time, covered me with security. I knew myself loved, even when no human being considered my need.' The cross became a symbol of ultimate victory to her.

In the late summer of 1944, she stood on the edge of the pavement at Treebeek in the south of Holland with thousands of others and cheered and waved at the columns of Allied tanks that set them all free from a vile tyranny. Though in a crowd, she felt alone. There was no Bastian Ader to thank. She had nowhere to go, no friends, no family, no money. There was no one close to her except the Christ she had come to know by faith.

Fortunately she found someone to take her in. She helped the Red Cross, and for the first time in her life began to attend church. She told the minister that she wanted to receive the bread and the wine at the communion service. Naturally the pastor was curious about her since she was Jewish by race and Christian by belief. She had come to believe that by turning to Christ, a Jew became spiritually complete. It was not a matter of being converted to a new religion, but fulfilling the old one by bringing it to completion. It seemed so clear to her that the Old Testament prophecies only had meaning as they came true in the

New Testament. As she would say in later years, she exchanged 'religion' for the reality of God.

Hansie Dobschiner told the Dutch Reformed minister in Treebeek the story of her spiritual journey. On Sunday, 19 November 1944, she was baptized. She knelt on a special stool in front of the assembled congregation. The minister said, 'Johanna-Ruth Dobschiner, I baptize you in the Name of the Father, the Son, and the Holy Spirit.' When the words 'Father, Son and Holy Spirit' were pronounced Hansie felt cold water on her forehead forming the shape of a cross. It was as if she was invisibly marked. To her it was an everlasting mark, which nobody else would ever see. After being baptized and confessing her faith, she received the bread and wine from the Lord's Table.

Soon after being received into the church, Hansie received the news from the north of Holland that Domie had been killed. Betrayed for money, he had been arrested in Haarlem. Taken to a Gestapo prison in Amsterdam, he was tortured, but did not betray a single name. He was shot there on Monday, 20 November 1944, aged only thirty-five. Hansie could scarcely take the news in. It seemed particularly poignant to her that his death came one day after her baptism and communion. A fine Christian man had lost his life just as all Holland was on the verge of liberation by the Allies. She wrote, 'He died to secure my life in this world. Christ died to secure it in the next. Life here and life eternal by the shedding of blood.'

When the Second World War ended Hansie was only twenty years old. It took her at least two years to recover from living like a hunted animal for so long. Though she never gave way to bitterness, self-pity, or the desire for recrimination which would have been so understandable, she had forgotten how to laugh or live a normal life.

In post-war Holland she was delighted to meet with other Jewish survivors of the Holocaust. When they found out that she accepted Jesus as the Messiah, they accused her of being a 'Geschmad'. This means an apostate from Judaism, a Jewish person who has been baptized into the Christian faith. The Jewish community would accept that a Jew could be an atheist, a Communist, even a criminal, but never a Christian. It was, and is, seen as betrayal. Though Hansie clung fervently to her Jewish roots and hated anti-Semitism, it made no difference. The Jewish community would not accept her. There is no place in Judaism for the 'Messianic Jew'.

Britain exercised a magnetic power on Hansie's mind, probably because it had stood out as a beacon of freedom during the years of war and tyranny. In 1946, sponsored by the generosity of the International Hebrew Christian Alliance, Hansie studied for two years at the Bible Training Institute in Glasgow. The training to qualify as a nurse took a further three years at Glasgow's Victoria Infirmary. The plan was to be a staff nurse at Tiberias Hospital in Israel. It was not to be. Instead, she married a Scotsman, so becoming Hansie Douglas. Twin girls were born soon after. At last she enjoyed a normal family life.

Hansie Douglas had a great gift for friendship, even with many German people. Tirelessly, she worked to foster good relations between Christians and Jews. Both Independent Television and the BBC—the latter in 1989—made documentaries about her. The cameras followed her as she retraced her steps to the house where she had once lived in Amsterdam, and from which her parents were so cruelly removed. She is seen on Amsterdam station reliving the scenes of the deportations, and in the attic where she peeled potatoes and became a Christian believer. The hero of the documentary has to be Bastian Johan Ader, 'Domie'. The pictures of her describing her memories of him while glancing down at his simple grave make compelling viewing. The gravestone just gives his name and two dates: 30–12–09 and 20–11–44.

When her husband Donald became a polio victim, he needed to be cared for twenty-four hours a day. With very little help, Hansie fulfilled the role of carer for many years. Her daughter Anne became a consultant psychiatrist in Glasgow. Dorothy married and went to live in Australia.

Hansie Douglas died of cancer in Glasgow in 2002 aged seventy-six. Her faith never changed from the basic beliefs that she had come to on Easter Monday 1944, though her understanding obviously increased. When she was puzzled for a title for her memories, her teenage children thought of 'Selected to Live'. The book *Selected to Live*, now translated into ten languages, has rarely been out of print since first published in 1969. It presents a vivid picture of Nazi-occupied Holland, and a gripping pen-portrait of a resilient young woman trying to avoid death as a consequence of one of the greatest crimes in history.

More information on Johanna-Ruth Dobschiner

For over thirty years I had the privilege of writing and speaking to Hansie Douglas. All the papers relevant to her wartime life were photocopied for me. The TV documentaries mentioned above are also sources for details of her life. These are the reasons why there is information in this account that is unique and additional to her other writings.

When *Selected to Live* went out of print, she was not happy, and was keen to see her book of memories available once again. She was not feeling well at the time and, through a friend within the firm, I encouraged her to approach Hodder Headline. In 2000 they reprinted it. The first copy in her possession was given to me as a Christmas present in 1999 with the inscription: 'Thank you for allowing the Lord to use you to bring this book back to life ...' Naturally, it is my hope that my readers will follow this account by reading *Selected to Live*.

Her obituary appeared in the *Glasgow Herald* on 17 August 2002 and added further minor details about her life story.

A book about the remarkable life of Bastian Ader is available only in Dutch. The details are: *Een Groninger Pastorie in de Storm* by J. A. Ader-Appels. Betty Holt, author of several books, has skilfully translated this book into English. It has not yet been published.

5

Charles Fraser-Smith

The man who was 'Q'

*Orders came initially by telephone ... With his
personal assistant listening in, he would hear,
'Is that CT6?' ... 'Yes,' he would say. Then
the voice on the other end would identify itself
by using a code name. There would follow a
description of what was wanted ... Secrecy
was paramount.*

Charles Fraser-Smith

5

Charles Fraser-Smith

'**P**ay attention, 007.'

'Sorry, "Q"; I was thinking about something else.'[1]

So runs part of a conversation between the fictitious secret agent James Bond and 'Q', code name for the clever maker of ingenious tricks and devices that Bond uses to outwit his enemies.

It was a series of action films that drew public attention to James Bond, or agent number '007'. These films were based on a character in a series of novels written by Ian Fleming between 1945 and his early death in 1964.

How did Fleming come to create his hero, Bond? Beyond any reasonable doubt Fleming's experiences as Personal Assistant to the Director of Naval Intelligence during World War II introduced him to real secret agents. These brave but little-known men and women provided him with the basic ideas for the character.

What of the origin of 'Q'? In the Bond stories 'Q' is a genius with gadgets. He is always bothered that the reckless James Bond will break his inventions, or not return them. In the war Fleming had access to a particular official working in the Ministry of Supply who was involved in this type of work. He knew that this man was arranging for specially made boxes of Dunlop golf balls to be sent to British prisoner-of-war camps. Some of the golf balls were no doubt used to amuse bored prisoners; some contained secret messages, maps and tiny compasses to help escape attempts. Fleming arranged to meet this man from the Ministry of Supply—Charles Fraser-Smith.

In Fleming's novel *Diamonds are Forever* a knife is used to open up a golf ball. Three uncut diamonds drop onto the surface of a desk. Years later, Fraser-Smith heard about the book and film and realized where the idea had its origin—in his office during World War II. The likeness between 'Q' in the Bond novels and Charles Fraser-Smith is very clear.

Bond's number, '007', derives from the way Naval Intelligence stored particular top-secret documents in a file marked 'NID/007'. The use of one thing for another purpose can be seen in 'Q' ships. When a warship was disguised as an unarmed freighter it was dubbed a 'Q' ship. 'Q' gadgets can be defined in the same way: objects with a disguised purpose, lifesaving or lethal.

During the war with Hitler's Germany there were many attempts to conceal items essential for certain operations behind enemy lines within everyday objects. Military men did most of this work. Fraser-Smith is probably unique because he was the only civilian involved in this aspect of the secret war. He worked for all the services, but was not attached to any in particular.

Nothing was known about Fraser-Smith's wartime activities until he was quizzed about them in 1977. His instinct had been to carry his secrets to the grave. It was pointed out that the Official Secrets Act imposed a thirty-year silence on him, but that period had elapsed. Even then, the true story had to be prised out of him bit by bit. Eventually the revelations were so interesting that he was persuaded to tell the story to a publisher. The result was the book *The Secret War of Charles Fraser-Smith* published in 1981. Its sub-title is 'The 'Q' Gadget Wizard of World War II'.

Although the book outlines most, but not all, of what he accomplished, he was disappointed that it did not mention his motivation and strong personal Christian faith. This is what provided direction, purpose and guidance for his decisions. There was much more to say, he thought. As a result, three further books from him followed in quick succession. One paid tribute to little-known heroes and heroines. It was entitled *Secret Warriors.* The next was called *Men of Faith.*

Then he wrote a book that outlined his heartfelt personal biblical faith, which was the driving force in not only what he had done in the conflict with Hitler's Germany, but for his whole life. Considering that he was nearing eighty years of age when his serious career as an author started, he was remarkably productive.

Charles Fraser-Smith was thirty-six when he started his important clandestine job in 1940. He signed the Official Secrets Act and was appointed as a temporary low-ranking civil servant in the Ministry of Supply Clothing and Textiles Department.

Photograph taken from Charles Fraser-Smith's official pass, 1942

Daily he commuted from the family home in Hertfordshire to his office in Portland House opposite St James's Park underground station, Westminster. The job was a cleverly thought-out pretence. Almost everybody else in the building had no idea what he was doing. He was outwardly insignificant, so it was not obvious that he had become production and procurement man to supply the armed forces and secret organizations. These included MI6 (Secret Intelligence Service), MI9 (Allied Prisoners of War: Escape and Evasion) and SOE (Special Operations Executive).

Many organizations and some individuals were involved in supplying the secret services and the armed forces, but Fraser-Smith made a distinctive and unusual contribution to the task. There was no job description and nobody ever told him what to do. He reckoned that fifty per cent of his orders came direct from intelligence organizations that knew precisely what they wanted; forty per cent went to departments that knew roughly what they wanted; and ten per cent were his own creations, developed and presented to an agency when he either knew or sensed that they had a need.

Orders came initially by telephone. There were three in the office: one for local calls, one for long-distance calls, and a red one for priority use. With his personal assistant listening in, he would hear, 'Is that CT6?' The speaker had reached Clothing and Textiles Department 6. 'Yes,' he would say.[2] Then the voice on the other end would identify itself by using a code name. There would follow a description of what was wanted. Sometimes a request was too complicated to be sorted out over the telephone. In that case a meeting would be set up in a local café, never at his office. Secrecy was paramount.

Charles Fraser-Smith developed contacts with 660 firms who produced the secret equipment and gadgets. His procedure was to carry copies of the Official Secrets Act with him. Usually only the managers and a few technical staff at the top of the firm would be involved. First, everybody involved was obliged to sign the Official Secrets Act. Most knew, or guessed, that they were being used to produce secret equipment. He made it a rule always to visit the firm, never vice-versa. Since he carried little official clout when approaching companies for help, he adopted an impressive manner and recalled that 'I always spoke as if I were Churchill himself.'[3] It helped to arrive in a car, so he had access to the car pool of his own Ministry of Supply, or the cars of the agency he was serving at the time.

Because secrecy was essential, hardly anything was written down. When the war was over, all he possessed were several gadgets, some of which are still in existence. There is also a book listing every order he made, the name and address and telephone number of the supplier, and the cost to the ministry. Every firm was listed in this one handwritten notebook. His son Brian counted them. That is how we know that the figure of 660 firms is accurate.

Charles Fraser-Smith had not been installed in his office long before he received a call from MI9 asking if it was possible to hide a small compass in a fountain pen. The first problem with this was that a compass small enough to hide in a pen did not exist. He tracked down a firm in the London borough of Clerkenwell that had a contract to build large compasses for the Royal Navy. The whole firm had no more than six employees and was owned by two brothers called Barker. When they heard the request, it was regarded as a challenge to their professional skills. The challenge was met: before long compasses of one quarter of an inch (6.35 mm.) in diameter were being mass-produced. For the pen he went to a firm called Mentmore Ltd in Platignum House. They

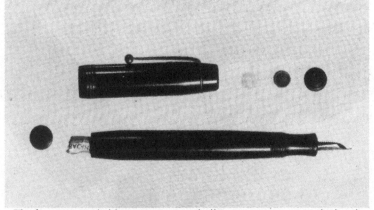

The fountain penheld a compass in a hollow compartment in the head. The mushroom-headed cap concealed the vital joint. Later the ink sac was reduced in size and a paper-thin map was secreted in the space gained.

eventually produced a fountain pen that had a half-size rubber ink sac. The space saved was filled with a silk-rag tissue map. The compass was hidden in the cap.

One of the most bizarre episodes of the war occurred in 1941 when Hitler's deputy, Rudolf Hess, flew to Britain without official German permission. After parachuting into Scotland, he was captured. While he was lying drugged in the Tower of London, MI5, the internal security service, asked Fraser-Smith to make a copy of his uniform. He arranged for Courtauld's experts in fabrics to match the cloth. The copy was made and delivered. No explanation for its possible use was offered, though various theories have been suggested. The British had already captured a lot of real German uniforms, which deepens the mystery about the purpose of copying Hess's uniform. Fraser-Smith knew that enemy uniforms served a wide range of purposes. There may be no connection with Hess, but the Long Range Desert Group operating behind enemy

*A box of 'Q' pencils, with the contents of one pencil displayed—
a small compass and a rolled up map of Germany.*

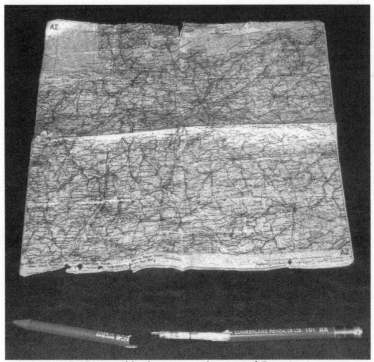

A 'Q' pencil broken to reveal a map of Germany.

lines in North Africa used German uniforms he supplied. This daring unit was the forerunner of Britain's most elite fighting force, the Special Air Service, or SAS.

Today, visitors to the Museum of the Cumberland Pencil Company at Keswick, in Cumbria, can see 'secret pencils'. When Fraser-Smith wanted pencils with secret compartments, he visited Keswick in 1942. Technical Manager Fred Tee and a few top department managers (out of the workforce of 140) signed the Official Secrets Act, headed home as normal at 17.30 and then sneaked back into the factory in the early evenings. Taking some finished green-painted pencils made of Kenya cedar, they drilled out most of the inside, starting from the top. Into the secret compartments went tightly rolled maps printed on non-rustling silk-rag tissue. A compass was then inserted before the rubber eraser was glued on. The 'Q' pencils marked 101 contained a general map of Germany. 102, 103 and 104 held maps displaying escape routes to the north, south and west of the country. Nobody will ever know how many airmen and others were helped by Keswick's secret pencils.

British national newspapers published on 20 November 1943 carried photographs of bomb-damaged Hamburg. They were taken at ground level by secret means. The Air Ministry requested the pictures and Fraser-Smith supplied the 'secret means'. This was the most effective miniature camera then available, the Minox. The cigarette lighter, common at the time, could be used as a hiding place for the Minox. Agents in Hamburg using the Minox had taken the pictures. Its film was about half the size of a postage stamp and fifty pictures could be taken on one roll of film. Kodak produced the film when requested by Fraser-Smith. Minox cameras were hard to find. One day he received an unexpected telephone call from a person who would not identify himself. The caller told him precisely where sixty Minox cameras were being held in secret. Fraser-Smith immediately arranged for the police at Scotland Yard to confiscate the cameras in the interest of the war effort.

A shaving brush with a secret compartment in the handle.

The problems with the Minox were not over. How was exposed film to be smuggled back into

Britain? His answer was the use of a torch with two batteries. A watertight container into which a film could be inserted replaced one of these batteries. The torch was made so that it gave light using one battery. In addition, he organized the manufacture of a shaving brush with a hollowed-out handle. A reverse thread protected the secret compartment, so if an attempt was made to unscrew the base in the normal manner, it just closed more tightly.

Hitler's fortifications were intended as protection against invasion from England. They were known as the 'Atlantic Wall'. Agents with Minox cameras secretly photographed them. The knowledge gained helped the soldiers who invaded Normandy on D-Day to know the obstacles they would have to face.

In late 1944 Germany deployed an early cruise missile called the V-1, or 'Doodlebug', which killed over 6,000 British civilians and injured nearly 18,000. Agents used the Minox camera to take pictures of their launch sites so that British bombers had a better chance of blowing them to pieces before the V-1s could be fired in the direction of London.

Major Pat Reid was one of the few who managed to escape from Colditz Castle prisoner-of-war camp. A filmed interview with him still exists in which he pays tribute to Fraser-Smith by name. There were many reasons for this. Charles had the sense never to use Red Cross parcels to smuggle helpful devices to prisoners in case the Nazis stopped these welcome packages. Coded messages were included in parcels from relatives to tell the Colditz men, and other prisoners, what to look out for. Innocent packets of handkerchiefs could become useful maps. Those to be used when 'on the run' showed a map of Germany when soaked in urine. A message saying, 'Do not eat the pink sweets,' indicated that sweets of this colour were to be dissolved in water to make a solution. When a linen or cotton handkerchief was put in the water a map showing escape routes would appear.

Gigli saws were made of interlaced cutting wire. Originally used

Dominoes sent to prisoners-of-war and SOE agents were useful carriers.

for brain surgery, Charles had them hardened so that they could be adapted to cut through metal bars. Their virtue was that they could be concealed in ordinary boot or shoelaces, around shaving mirrors or in the tops of tins. Smokers' pipes, which were quite common in those days, were fitted out with asbestos linings to protect maps hidden inside. Dominoes and chessmen could be filled with helpful items, including ink used for forging documents.

In 1943 Fraser-Smith received an order for a metal box with a difference. Metal boxes to hold guns and ammunition were often supplied, knowing that they would be dropped by parachute to shadowy organizations in Europe. This one had to be just over six feet long, three feet wide (approximately 1. 80 m. by 90 cm.) and have a valve and vacuum pump. A life jacket nicknamed the Mae West was included in the order. Charles did not have a clue what he was involved in until the truth emerged after the war. Into the box went the corpse of an unknown man who had died from pneumonia. Documents designed to deceive enemy agents were placed on the body of 'Major Martin'. Officers of a British submarine then released the body from the box at a predetermined spot, knowing that it would be washed up on a Spanish beach. At the time Spain had a fascist government sympathetic to Hitler, so it was reasonable to guess that the Spanish would give the false information to the Germans.

The ruse succeeded. Hitler was tricked into believing that the Allies would invade Kalamata and Cape Araxos in Greece, and possibly Sardinia too. As a result he moved soldiers to Greece. The real intention was to invade Sicily and to divert attention away from the very obvious preparations. The story is told in the book and film called *The Man Who Never Was*.

Charles Fraser-Smith also experimented with concentrated foodstuffs. Chivers supplied potato powder and he persuaded Coty, the cosmetics firm, to make it into cubes. Though less than delicious, the results found their way into escape packs. Forces like the Chindits operating behind Japanese lines necessarily used concentrated foodstuffs. Another idea was to put concentrated condensed milk into tubes normally used for toothpaste. Nestlé was the firm most successfully used for this project. The tube-makers produced millions of these items and Nestlé filled them with various concentrated milk products. Probably the most popular concentrated product was a malted milk tablet made by Horlicks. The taste was good compared with other similar products. Horlicks tablets went into thousands of escapers' and evaders' kits.

Equipping male and female agents who were parachuted into occupied Europe by Special Operations Executive was a huge task. The poisons and explosives they carried were not Fraser-Smith's concern. Other matters were. Great care was taken to ensure that clothing and personal effects in their pockets looked precisely like those to be found in the country where they operated. An example of his work was asking Bryant and May, the matchmakers, to produce perfect copies of foreign matchboxes. The British and American Tobacco Company made all the foreign cigarettes that were supplied to agents operating in enemy territory. It must be remembered that smoking was far more common in the war years than now. Elizabeth Arden produced all the foreign make-up for female operatives. The firm which printed UK banknotes, Waterlow, counterfeited foreign money for the use of agents. Those arrested could try to eat messages if they were written on Fraser-Smith rice paper.

Soon after the United States joined the struggle against the Nazis, President Franklin Roosevelt gave King George VI a gift, which the king passed to the Ministry of Supply to assess its usefulness. At first glance it appeared to be a pocket-sized camera. However, if the shutter button was pressed, a tiny radio played. Before long, Charles Fraser-Smith arranged for the miniature radio to be reduced to half its size. Eighty-volt long-life batteries were manufactured to power it. Many suitable innocent-looking tins contained the result: the widely used 'Q' radio.

The examples of Fraser-Smith's activities given here hardly scratch the surface. At his busiest he reckoned he dealt with about 100 telephone calls a day. For all the interest and excitement of his work, and the ingenuity with which he discharged it, he took the Christian view of war. 'Only fools and barbarians glorify war,' he used to say. 'Fighting an aggressor is a sad and uncomfortable task … but it has to be done when there is no alternative.'[4] It was the comment of a Christian man who found himself plunged into the murky world of tricks and deception. Everything he did in the struggle with Hitler's Germany was done as a Christian. Even small decisions were the result of prayer. His personal relationship with God governed all his actions as he fought his secret war.

One of four children, Charles Fraser-Smith was born in 1904. Orphaned at the age of five, his upbringing became the responsibility of a well-to-do aunt and uncle in Hertfordshire. It was a devout household. After breakfast all work ceased. The maids and the gardener joined the family in fervent family prayers. Charles could recall foreign missionaries being prayed for, which may partly explain a later event in his life. Eventually he was

Miniature radios, complete with tiny earphones and an eighty-volt long-life battery, were housed in flat metal boxes commonly in use for packs of fifty cigarettes, or in tins disguised as lunch boxes. The box containing the radio was 1¾ inches (4.45 cm.) deep and 6 inches (15 cm.) square.

sent to Brighton College, a fee-paying boarding school, where he proved 'scholastically useless except for woodwork, science and making things'.[5]

In his mid-teens he found himself on Littlehampton beach during the family holiday. In a letter to the author he describes the sand hockey and a crowd of boys gathering to hear the gospel of Christ in the evening. It was not unlike the modern beach missions still to be seen at some seaside resorts in summer months. It was during that ever-memorable fortnight that he gave up 'religion'. He described 'religion' as trying to earn God's forgiveness by being outwardly good. In place of this he committed his life to Christ. For him, the change brought by conversion to Christ was dramatic and had permanent effects. It was an inward, spiritual new birth. It resulted in a sincere grief for sin and an experience of the love of God. It gave him a personal faith in Christ as the perfect Son of God, who died and rose again to save sinners.

At seventeen he confirmed the change in his life by being baptized at Cholmeley Hall, an Open Brethren church in Highgate. The same year he left school and spent a year 'teaching' at a preparatory school in Portsmouth. His clearest memories of this school were giving lessons in photography, wiring the buildings with electric bells and showing intrigued boys how guns worked, using gunpowder and strong metal tubing. His guardians now suggested medicine—the route his elder brother Alfred had taken—but Charles was drawn to agriculture. Three years were spent working on a Littlehampton farm. During this time his faith in the Lord matured. He taught regularly in young people's Bible classes but, as his brother commented, he was no preacher. His training in agriculture ended in 1925.

When he expressed an interest in missionary work in the French protectorate of Morocco, his guardians sent him to the Institut Biblique in Paris to gain fluency in French and more detailed knowledge of the Scriptures.

In Paris he met Admiral Dalencourt, who influenced him in several ways. One thing Charles never forgot was being given the admiral's motto: 'Sans Dieu—rien' ('Without God—nothing', or 'Without God all is nothing'). This was explained in part of a long manuscript Charles sent to the writer of this book:

'There is no true meaning in life without God. The universe is incomprehensible and man a purposeless accident without a Creator. We must seek to be made God-centred. I soon added to the motto "Sans Bible—rien". The Bible is the only authoritative guide in life. We should place ourselves under the authority of the Word of God. I always find that directly one gets slack concerning Bible reading and study, faith is weakened. Also, we are to be "doers of the Word", not merely hearers. My second addition to the Admiral's motto is "Sans Christ—rien". The Bible states that mankind deserves to be separated from a holy God because of his self-centred sin. This sin creates a barrier between God and us just as it does in ordinary human relationships. God sent his Son, Jesus Christ, to pay the penalty we deserve for our sin. The innocent one died for the guilty. Three days after his sacrifice, he completed his work by conquering death itself. I believe in the experience of being a new person in Christ, receiving him as Saviour, knowing him as Lord and serving him.'

Passionately desiring to be a missionary, Charles went to Morocco in 1926. He supported himself by farming and trading. He proved to be a quick learner, an improviser, introducing new ploughs, irrigation schemes and proper fertilization. Every spare minute was spent learning Arabic because the world of Islam was all around him.

His life in Morocco began by running a farm between Marrakesh and the Atlas mountains. By the age of twenty-four he was manager of the farmlands and estates of the Moroccan royal family. The sultan's fertile land was jealously protected. Neither the French government nor any European had ever been permitted to buy an acre of land anywhere near it. Eventually he left the sultan's service with regret on both sides.

After his marriage to Blanche, who was a missionary working in Casablanca, he delegated the management of his other farming enterprises and turned to organizing an orphanage in Marrakesh.

It would be fair to say that Charles did nothing but good for Morocco although, as usual in Muslim lands, lasting converts to the Christian faith were few. At the time of writing one of his original enterprises, the orphanage, has passed to the control of the Save the Children Fund, which cares for more than 100 disabled children on what was once his farm.

1940 was a year full of grim world news. In June, France surrendered to the seemingly unstoppable German forces. The French governor of Morocco, General Noguès, was a fascist supporter of the Germans. Charles Fraser-Smith had no intention of helping to grow food that could be sent to support 'Vichy' France. To the embarrassment of many loyal French people, this southern part of France willingly cooperated with the Nazi forces occupying the north and the west coast of France. As a result he made his way to Casablanca, looking for a way to escape with his wife and son, Brian. A Norwegian freighter, S.S. *Varenberg*, brought them to safety in Britain. Liverpool was a welcome sight. All he had to show outwardly for fourteen years in Morocco was a few French francs amounting to thirty pounds in British money.

Soon after this, the government directed him to work at a comparatively unimportant job in the Avro aircraft factory in Leeds. One Sunday he attended the Open Brethren evangelical church as usual and at an after-church meeting was invited to describe his missionary work in Morocco. Among those listening were Bible scholar and prolific author Professor F. F. Bruce, Sir George Oliver, Director General of the Ministry of Supply, and George Ritchie Rice, who was in charge of the local office of the same ministry. Charles described what he had done in some detail, unwittingly giving a compelling picture of his inventiveness, initiative and self-reliance.

The men from the Ministry of Supply must have been impressed because on the next day he was offered 'a funny sort of job'. He would have to sign the Official Secrets Act and move to London.

His instructions were simply that 'You will be supplying our forces with "various requirements".' The rest is history.

With the war over, his health deteriorated. He had worked without holidays and under stress for too long. At least he had the consolation of knowing that his actions had saved many lives. Though his heart was still in Morocco, he could not have returned if he had wanted to. The Muslim government banned Christian missionaries from post-war Morocco. As a result, he bought a derelict farm in north Devon and restored it to prosperity. He was an early convert to organic principles in farming.

His first wife died in 1965. Later he married the talented Lin, who lovingly and loyally supported his Christian activities. He was a life-member of the Bible Society, an active member of the Gideons, the organization that places free Bibles in hospitals, schools and elsewhere. Charles and Lin personally placed Bibles in many of Devon's hotels and bed-and-breakfast houses. He gave unstinting support to nephew Keith Fraser-Smith, an Anglican minister whose heart is in missions to North Africa. Profits from his books mostly went to this cause.

After the publication of *The Secret War of Charles Fraser-Smith* he became a minor celebrity. He appeared on several radio programmes, and TV documentaries were produced about him and his 'Q' gadgets. In these appearances he tried to point out that the real 'Q' had been a Christian.

Personally, Charles had found Ian Fleming charming and persuasive, not unlike the character of Bond in some ways. However, he was not happy with Fleming's attitude to women, as displayed in Bond's actions in the books and films. Nevertheless, Charles was generous in his praise of Fleming when he mentioned him. He wrote, 'Fleming was the type we needed to win the Second World War. Thankfully, that war brought in all kinds of geniuses.'[6]

To say that Charles Fraser-Smith lived a full life is an

understatement. Probably because he was unconventional and never had much time for accepted ways of doing things, he made an impact on everybody who knew him. He had boundless energy and total Christian commitment.

When he died aged eighty-eight in November 1992, some comments he had written about death were read at his funeral at his request: 'I always think of death not as a sunset, an ending, but as a sunrise, a beginning ... death for the true follower of Christ, is entrance to real life. This starts at the "death of the cross" ... it is the greatest event in life, the climax of life ... the entrance into something magnificent. It is the beginning of true and perfect living. We can say with Paul, "For me to live is Christ, but to die is gain." In this way, "Death is swallowed up in victory."'[7]

More information on Charles Fraser-Smith

Charles Fraser-Smith answered my questions about his faith and wartime activities during correspondence over many years. Since his death, his wife Lin has been extremely helpful, providing information and unique video cassettes of his TV appearances.

In addition to *The Secret War of Charles Fraser-Smith* (Michael Joseph, 1981), Paternoster published four books. The three written by Charles Fraser-Smith are called *Secret Warriors* (1984), *Men of Faith* (1986) and *Four Thousand Year War* (1988). The last title gives a detailed account of his Christian beliefs. The last Paternoster title is David Porter's biography of Charles Fraser-Smith (1989).

Grateful thanks are expressed to David Tee of Keswick who provided the information concerning, and photographs of, the 'Q' pencils. For anybody interested in the production of the unique pencils, a visit to the museum of the Cumberland Pencil Company in Keswick, England, would prove very rewarding.

Grateful thanks too to Brian Fraser-Smith, who inherited 100 of his father's gadgets and the original order book. He has been a mine of information and photographs.

Some of the gadgets are displayed at the Tangmere Military Aviation Museum, West Sussex, and others at the National Motor Museum, Beaulieu, Hampshire. Both these museums are in southern England.

There are two professionally produced DVDs available. They are:

1. The Secret Life of Charles Fraser-Smith.

2. The Wartime Gadgets of Charles Fraser-Smith.

Any reader who found this chapter interesting will be fascinated by the DVDs.

6

Mitsuo Fuchida

Chief pilot at Pearl Harbor

*Like a hurricane out of nowhere, 360 torpedo
planes, bombers and fighters attacked and
temporarily shattered American naval power
in the Pacific. The man who led the assault
on Pearl Harbor was ... Mitsuo Fuchida. In
his 'Kate' bomber, he was first over the target
and the last to leave it.*

*Mitsuo Fuchida in later life, pictured during
a preaching engagement at Pearl Harbor*

6

Mitsuo Fuchida

Sunday, 7 December 1941, started out like a normal day for the men of the American Pacific Fleet, which was lying peacefully at anchor in Pearl Harbor, Hawaii.

Without declaring war the Japanese surprised the American defences with a carrier-launched air raid in the early morning. Like a hurricane out of nowhere, 360 torpedo planes, bombers and fighters attacked and temporarily shattered American naval power in the Pacific. The man who led the assault on Pearl Harbor was thirty-nine-year-old Mitsuo Fuchida. In his 'Kate'[1] bomber, he was first over the target and the last to leave it. It was Fuchida who gave the orders, 'To! To! To!' ('Attack!' or 'Charge!') and 'Tora! Tora! Tora!' (the code word to signal the achievement of total surprise). That one attack unleashed the fury of death and destruction that engulfed the Far East as part of World War II.

Having observed the devastation, Fuchida was full of pride. He was later to write, 'My heart was filled with joy at my success … It was the most thrilling exploit of my career.'[2] Years would pass before he understood that he had left behind more than smashed battleships and aircraft and over 3,000 US dead. He also left

A Japanese Nakajima B5N ('Kate') as used by Mitsuo Fuchida in the raid on Pearl Harbor. The 'Kate' was a small, carrier-based plane, not a big, heavy bomber.

behind a nation that would not rest until Japan paid in full for that morning's work. It was also as a direct result of the unprovoked raid on Pearl Harbor that the US joined Britain and its allies in the war against Hitler's Germany. Fuchida had awakened a sleeping giant.

On his return to Japan Fuchida was given the privilege of explaining to Emperor Hirohito the details of the Pearl Harbor attack. He was a confident speaker. The emperor was impressed. As he left Hirohito's presence, Fuchida's head was in the clouds at the honour he had been given. Everywhere he went in Japan he was treated as a hero and idolized. After all, he was one of Japan's most experienced naval pilots.

Though only small in stature, he was a hard man with a strong personality. An observant Japanese news cameraman had unspoken nicknames for all the senior officers. Fuchida's was 'Hitler'. In 1941 Fuchida had a genuine admiration for Hitler and had even grown a toothbrush moustache in imitation of his hero.

Born in 1902 in an isolated Japanese rural community, Fuchida was one of a family of five children. 'Mitsuo' means 'number three boy'. He had two older brothers and two younger sisters. His father, a teacher, noticed early that Mitsuo was a natural leader.

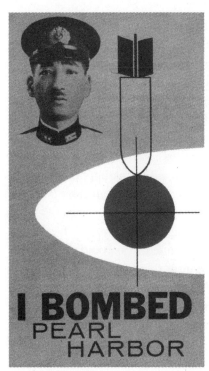

Front page of a tract written by Fuchida in 1950, showing his moustache copied in admiration of Hitler

'I always loved to be out of doors with the neighbourhood children,' Mitsuo remembered. 'They always chose me as their chief when we staged mock battles, or when we hunted hares in winter.'[3]

Influenced by the increasingly military atmosphere and his father's nationalism, Fuchida entered Etajima naval academy when he was nineteen. Many young men caught the aviation 'bug' between the world wars. He had his first flight in his second year at Etajima, went solo after only fourteen hours instruction, and so began the climb to having the immense total of about 10,000 hours in the air recorded in his log book.

By that momentous December day in 1941, Fuchida was a married man with two children. He drank a lot, smoked heavily and, although basically irreligious, gave outward support to Shinto, the Japanese state religion. Nor was he inexperienced in attacking helpless targets from the air. In 1937 he had given obedient and thoughtless support to the war Japan had started against China. Based at Nanking in mainland China, he had led frequent bombing missions against the Chinese.

After Pearl Harbor he saw widespread action. He led a raid on a British base in Ceylon that sank the carrier *Hermes*. Another

mission damaged the town of Darwin on the northern coast of
Australia. During the battles for Java, Fuchida's plane was hit
and had to make a crash-landing in the Borneo jungle. His radio
operator died instantly. Fuchida crawled from the battered wreck
unhurt. Nothing seemed to stop the torrent of Japanese victories.
They became smug and overconfident.

Just before the Battle of Midway in June 1942, Fuchida had an
operation for appendicitis on board his aircraft carrier, the *Akagi*.
He was ashamed at the thought of missing this important battle,
largely because he was the overall commander of all the planes on
four carriers.

Disobeying doctor's orders, he struggled from the sick bay below
Akagi's waterline up to the deck. The least he could do, he felt,
was to encourage his men by waving to them as they took off.
Unknown to the Japanese, the Americans had broken the enemy's
codes and knew their plans beforehand. In the middle of some
fierce fighting, a squadron of American Dauntless dive-bombers hit
Akagi with their bombs.

Had he not been up on deck, Fuchida would have been burned
alive with the thirty men trapped by twisted metal in *Akagi's* sick
bay. Even on the deck there was chaos as flames leapt high. A
thunderous explosion hurled Fuchida nearly ten feet (six metres)
into the air. The crunching fall broke both his legs. Already
weak after the operation, he was reduced to crawling to safety.
Fire singed his clothing. At a critical moment two men raced
by and recognized him. His rescuers put him in a net sling and
lowered him into a small boat. Taken to a ship that had escaped
the American onslaught, Fuchida had the miserable experience
of seeing the carrier that he had once used as a base to launch
the attack on Pearl Harbor now reduced to a sinking wreck. The
Japanese Navy lost four carriers that day. The Battle of Midway
turned the course of the Pacific war in America's favour.

Fuchida would recover from his injuries and near-death

experience, but Japan would never recover completely from the results of the Battle of Midway. After getting better from the worst of his wounds, Fuchida was appointed to the Naval War College in Tokyo. One of his duties in that post was to research why the Midway struggle had been an American victory. He interviewed dozens of officers and had access to confidential Japanese files. Fuchida drafted the final report.

In the early 1950s, with Masatake Okumiya, he co-authored a book called *Midway, the Battle that Doomed Japan*. This has remained the standard basic book of reference giving the Japanese perspective. It has been in print almost continuously. It reveals another side of Fuchida—his fine analytical mind.

Fully recovered, he became a staff officer with duties such as training replacement naval airmen. By 1944 he was in charge of all air operations of the Japanese Combined Fleet, the highest appointment open to a naval flyer. Promoted to captain, he found himself restless in a desk job. His brain was saying, 'Make peace'; his instinct countered with 'Fight to the end'.

On 5 August 1945 he attended a conference at Hiroshima the day before the American B-29 bomber dropped the first atom bomb on the town. Unexpectedly an order came telling him to go to another base for discussions. At 17.00 the day before Hiroshima was destroyed, Fuchida climbed into a navy plane and flew himself out of the area.

In the days following the explosion, Fuchida returned to Hiroshima as one of the investigating team. For three days they walked round the ruins with no protective outfits, just ordinary uniforms. When he looked back on his time at Hiroshima, he found it hard to understand why almost all of the seventy men involved died soon afterwards from radiation, yet he survived in perfect health. It is not surprising that he considered that 'some greater force' must be protecting him.

At the end of the war the Americans forced the Japanese

leadership to sign a humiliating surrender on the deck of the battleship USS *Missouri*. Watching from an upper deck was the disheartened Captain Mitsuo Fuchida. He pondered: he had been present at the start of the war as well as at its formal end. Between those two events most of his friends had been killed in horrendous ways. He wasn't the only surviving airman from Pearl Harbor, but he was the only survivor of seven commanders and thirty-two squadron leaders.

After the defeat he became bitter and disillusioned. He drank excessively and had a very serious moral lapse, which in different circumstances could have wrecked his marriage. He became a farmer and started to have his first thoughts about God as Creator. He penned a book called *No More Pearl Harbor* during which it occurred to him that the mess the world was in was due to human nature. But this thought haunted him: 'Who can change people?'

He talked to Japanese prisoners who were returning home from the US. 'How were you treated?' he would ask. Always the answer was: 'Well.' Several of his friends related the story of Peggy Covell, a young lady who visited and cared for Japanese prisoners. 'Why are you so kind to us?' they wanted to know. The reply was: 'Because Japanese soldiers killed my parents.' It turned out that her parents had been Christian missionaries who had been captured and beheaded as spies. Peggy was convinced that her parents would have forgiven their executioners before death. Could she do less? So she volunteered to work with Japanese prisoners of war. Fuchida was very impressed by this story, which exhibited grace and goodness that his Shintoism could not embrace.

Then, in 1948, Timothy Peitsch, a missionary, gave him a tract on Tokyo railway station. It was about how an American prisoner of the Japanese called Jacob DeShazer had become a Christian and forgiven the cruelties he had endured after reading the Bible and receiving Christ as his Saviour.

As a result Fuchida bought a New Testament. Before

he had covered thirty pages his mind was strangely impressed and captivated. He read Luke's Gospel and, in the story of the crucifixion, came to Christ's prayer: 'Father, forgive them, for they do not know what they are doing' (Luke 23:34). It dawned on him that this was the source for the love displayed by Peggy Covell and Jacob DeShazer.

Later Fuchida was to write about the resulting spiritual experience in these words: 'I was impressed that I was one of those for whom Christ had prayed those words. The many men I had killed had been slaughtered in the name of patriotism, because I did not understand the love that Christ wishes to implant within every heart. Right at the moment I read that prayer, I seemed to meet Jesus for the first time. I understood the meaning of his death as a substitute for my wickedness, and so, in prayer I requested him to forgive my sins and change me from a bitter disillusioned ex-pilot into a well-balanced Christian with purpose in living. That date, 14 April 1950, is the day I became a new person. My complete view of life was changed by the intervention of Christ.'[4] At the time of his personal conversion to Christ, Mitsuo Fuchida was already forty-seven years old.

Media reaction was not slow in coming. 'Pearl Harbor Hero Converts to Christianity' was one typical headline. Men who had fought for Japan wanted him to give up 'this crazy idea'. An ex-flyer named Noboru Nakamura took it further. He came to Fuchida's home. The moment they were alone, he drew out an ornate knife. With the point against Fuchida's throat, he cried, 'I looked up to you, and now I must kill you.'[5] Fuchida told him the story about how he had become a Christian in his farmhouse without knowing one other Christian in the world. He had simply prayed as the Bible described. They spoke for three hours. At first the knife pricked Fuchida's throat; then slowly it was put down. The would-be assassin had been a member of a suicide unit and had an artificial leg. He left pondering Fuchida's personal testimony to the life-changing power of the Word of God.

Five years later Fuchida preached in a church at Amagasaki. There in the congregation was the one-time kamikaze pilot, now an elder of the church.

However, it was some time before Fuchida fully realized the moral and practical implications of being a real Christian. Part of the problem was that he had never possessed an Old Testament and had no understanding of the law, such as the Ten Commandments. Also, over-enthusiastic American missionaries to Japan told him to witness to crowds immediately. Trusting their judgement, he allowed himself to be pushed into prominence. It was a mistake. He had not yet attended any regular Christian worship or received any systematic Bible teaching. But as he read the Bible his life changed. His wife, Haruko, a Buddhist, watched him closely. To her surprise his open sins began to fall away. The hard drinker chose the safer option, total abstinence. He broke free from tobacco. Contact was made with Pastor Toshio Saito, an educated Presbyterian, who baptized him at Osaka Presbyterian Church in March 1951.

Haruko, their son Yoshiya (who called himself 'Joe') and daughter Miyako were so impressed that they freely attended worship. One by one they were converted and subsequently baptized by Pastor Saito. The conversion of his family also stood the test of time. In the strange providence of God both his son and daughter made new lives for themselves in the United States. Joe became an architect but, more importantly, both of them became zealous Christian believers in their adopted land.

In 1952 the Japanese government put real temptation in Fuchida's way. He was offered a top-level post as chief of staff in Japan's new Self-Defence Air Force. With his background he could have had high rank, regular income and public prestige. In 1957 the test was repeated: would he take the position of Minister of

Defence? The opportunities were given serious consideration. His reply was that he was convinced that he could best serve Japan, and all humanity, by being an ambassador for Christ. His calling was to be a full-time evangelist.

In this capacity he would criss-cross the world, visiting hundreds of cities and preaching thousands of gospel messages. He said, 'I think only of glorifying Christ, praising him, and serving him … The important thing is to preach Christ both in season and out of season.'[6] And he meant it. The world was his parish. His name and the nature of what he had done guaranteed that there were always more opportunities to preach than he could meet. This was particularly true in the United States. The attack on Pearl Harbor was a pivotal event in American history that was never going to be forgotten quickly.

When Fuchida learned that Jacob DeShazer was in Japan as a missionary, it was only natural that he would want to meet him. After all, DeShazer's story had been the substance of the Christian pamphlet that he had been given on Tokyo railway station. DeShazer had been a bombardier on the American revenge attack for Pearl Harbor, the Doolittle Raid of 1942. DeShazer's plane had bombed its targets on the Japanese mainland, and then crashed in part of China occupied by Japan. He had been taken prisoner and badly tortured. It was a high point in the lives of both men when the Doolittle raider shook hands with the Pearl Harbor commander. Together they were the embodiment of how real faith in Christ changes lives and makes former enemies into the best of friends. They prayed together and were destined to do gospel work with each other.

In 1952 Fuchida's schedule took him to DeShazer's home church, the First Methodist Church in Salem, Oregon. After preaching he had the pleasure of meeting DeShazer's mother, Mrs Hulda Andrus. This godly woman had prayed for her son's salvation and safety all the time he had been a prisoner. So, as

Fuchida reflected, this woman's prayers resulted in a tract being written by her son; this led to Fuchida's conversion, and now here he was in their home church. It seemed a strange cycle of events. 'How unpredictable and wonderful is the providence of God!' was the inevitable thought that came to him.

Fuchida returned to Pearl Harbor several times as an evangelist. There was always opposition from those Americans unwilling to forgive, and there was always support from those who wanted to move on from 1941. They could believe him when he said, 'I would give anything to retract my actions at Pearl Harbor, but it is impossible. Instead, I now work at striking the death blow to the basic hatred which infests the human heart and causes such tragedies. That hatred cannot be uprooted without assistance from Jesus Christ. He was the only one who was powerful enough to change my life and inspire it with his thoughts.'[7]

Often his schedule was too full. Living out of a suitcase and preaching regularly exhausts young men, never mind a man who was only converted when past middle age. When Fuchida was in Hawaii in 1953 addressing a group of Chinese people, he collapsed in front of them from nothing more serious than extreme tiredness. On another occasion a year or two later he was laid low for a while by physical exhaustion and inability to speak.

In the winter of 1954 Fuchida's programme took him to Tampa in Florida. One of America's pioneer airmen from the interwar years, Eugene Horle, noticed an advertisement in a newspaper that Fuchida would be preaching in a local church. Normally nothing would induce Horle to set foot in a church. The attraction of hearing an airman of roughly his own age was too much. Fuchida's message moved Horle, and he asked to meet him personally. As a result Horle found a new dimension in his life—personal faith in Christ. Later Horle wrote about his conversion. He commented: 'All the thrills of flying do not compare with the joy of knowing the Creator of the skies as Saviour and Lord.'[8] And he was quick to point out that the man God used to point him to Christ was Mitsuo Fuchida.

Much of Fuchida's time was given to evangelistic work in Japan. He was rightly suspicious of outward shows of conversion because he knew from experience that many could claim that they were 'converted' when they were not. At one point in 1955 he calculated that he had preached at 600 meetings to at least 200,000 people. Before he would accept that professions of faith were genuine he always waited for men and women to join a church and be baptized. By December 1955 he had received 568 such notifications from a wide variety of churches.

One of his campaigns was in Fukuoka on the Japanese island of Kyushu. The pastor of one church in the city wrote to him to say that the usual Sunday attendance had been no more than fifty. After two missions by Fuchida in October 1953 and February 1954 church membership had risen to over 200. After a meeting at Okayama, one of the local pastors wrote that sixty new people were attending the church, all of whom were baptized. All the evidence is that Fuchida was effective as a missionary.

This was reinforced after preaching in a prison in Fukuoka. After leaving the premises he was informed that twenty convicted murderers had not been allowed to attend the service. So he made arrangements to go back to preach to these doomed men. He spoke for an hour. All references to the war and his part in it were cut out. He went straight to his main point: Christ's concern for sinners, his compassion for the lost. He stressed that Christ had died, was crucified between two criminals, and how he had promised the penitent thief who acknowledged him as Lord: 'Today you will be with me in paradise' (Luke 23:43).

The men took his message to heart, and every one of them dropped to his knees to ask Christ's pardon for sin. In the period before their execution, Fuchida later found out that they had banded themselves together in what they called 'the Calvary

Club'. They gave one another help and consolation. The prison governor reported that usually the guards had to drag condemned men to the scaffold. Then he added: 'But the members of the Calvary Club walked to the gallows upright and straight, praying every step of the way, "Christ be with me today in paradise."'[9]

In 1958 Pastor Sakuramachi, who led a church in the Osaka slums, invited Fuchida to preach at a service. He reminded his guest of a time when the latter had spoken at another prison in Japan a few years earlier. Fuchida had a clear recollection of the lack of interest in the gospel on that occasion. The pastor revealed that he had been one of the prisoners who had heard his message. It had stimulated him to investigate the Christian faith, and as a result he had been converted.

During Fuchida's extensive European tour in the early 1960s he went to Hamburg. Paul Taylor, one of his fellow missioners to Hamburg in 1961, recorded his impressions of Fuchida in a letter to the author. He wrote, 'He was serenely without fear. Prisoners would pay careful attention when a man with Fuchida's credentials stood to speak. He had a charming and friendly disposition ... the grace of God had so obviously won his heart ... I remember him above all for his passionate love for Christ. He was manifestly devoted to making Jesus Christ known as often as he could, and to whoever would listen.'

In that spirit Mitsuo Fuchida laboured on until his death in Japan from the complications of diabetes in May 1976. He was seventy-three.

In a letter to the author at the time, Jacob DeShazer commented:

'My friend Mitsuo Fuchida will be enjoying heaven.' Through the grace of God alone the pilgrim had reached his ultimate destination.

More information on Mitsuo Fuchida

Mitsuo Fuchida wrote a number of tracts and booklets. The first was *I Bombed Pearl Harbor*, a leaflet published by the Pocket Testament League. Others are *From Pearl Harbor to Calvary* (Bible Literature International) and *I led the Air Attack on Pearl Harbor*.

Thurston Clarke refers to him in *Pearl Harbor Ghosts*. Elizabeth Sherrill contributed an article to *Guideposts* magazine called 'I'll Never Forget You—Mitsuo Fuchida'. When Fuchida came to London for the showing of *Tora! Tora! Tora!* Gordon Fyles interviewed him extensively. Don Mainprize wrote a summary of his life for the issue of *Power for Living* dated 1 December 1991.

Ken Anderson Films produced *One Came Back*, showing aspects of his life, particularly a return visit to Pearl Harbor in later years. The Cassell Military Paperback called *Midway*, by Fuchida and Okumiya, contains a lengthy personalized account by Fuchida of his activities up to and during that battle.

Gordon W. Prange, who knew Fuchida, has been fortunate in having Katherine V. Dillon and Donald M. Goldstein as his collaborators. At least six important books owe their existence to these authors. One is *God's Samurai*, a biography of Fuchida (Brassey's US, Inc.). My copy was a gift from DeShazer. Prange is excellent for historical background.

Internet articles should be checked for accuracy by referring to Fuchida's own works.

I would like to thank Paul S. Taylor of Lutterworth, England, for his clear word picture of Fuchida at Hamburg, written at my request.

7

Jacob DeShazer

Doolittle raider

and missionary to Japan

> The eighty airmen knew that, even if they
> could get airborne from the Hornet's deck in
> land-based bombers, there was no question
> of returning to it. After bombing Japan, they
> must fly on until they reached China. Much
> of China was in Japanese hands, so it was a
> high-risk operation.

Jacob DeShazer

7

Jacob DeShazer

Six hundred miles off the coast of Japan, the wind was driving the rain at twenty-seven knots along the deck of the aircraft carrier USS *Hornet*.

Sixteen North American B-25B Mitchell medium bombers stood, some with propellers spinning, ready for take off. Inside each of the twin-engine, twin-tailed aircraft a five-man crew waited tensely for the signal to go.

In the perspex nose of the last aircraft was twenty-nine-year-old Corporal Jacob DeShazer, the bombardier. It was 18 April 1942. The mission about to be launched would change the whole course of his life in ways he could never have imagined.

DeShazer had volunteered to fly on a one-off hazardous mission. Before the eighty men involved took off their commander, Lieutenant Colonel Doolittle, had promised a reunion of those who survived. As a result, on 18 April every year, the survivors meet together. In 1959 eighty silver goblets were presented, one for each man. Their names are engraved twice: the right way up and upside down. The goblets of the dead are upside down. With nobody else present except the raiders, one survivor lifts his goblet and proposes a toast: 'To those who have gone.' If a man has died in the preceding year, his goblet is turned over. After that, the roll of the dead is read out slowly.

The men who pay this tribute to their departed comrades are members of a group nobody else can join.Except their leader, all were in their twenties and thirties in April 1942, so by the law of nature reunions and the goblet ceremonies will cease in the early part of the twenty-first century. When the last goblet is turned over, the set will be displayed in a museum.

Though the men of the Doolittle Raid inevitably fade away, their mission will always be remembered in the annals of US military history for its courage and daring. This is the story of one of them, Jacob DeShazer, 'Jake' to his friends.

Jake was born in 1912 into a devout Christian family, which lived in Salem, Oregon, in the United States. His early life was unremarkable. His father died when he was two and his mother remarried. Hiram Andrus, his stepfather, was a farmer and a good example. Jake went to the Free Methodist Sunday school and church, but religion meant little to him. Everybody knew him as a rebel. He skipped school, thieved and became bored with small-town life.

Fully-grown, he was five feet six tall (1.67 metres), sturdy, and keen to make his own way in the world. The only work civilian life offered at the time was a series of unsatisfying dead-end jobs. However, the US Army Air Force offered security and good pay. So he signed on.

It was 1940 and America was at peace. The events of Pearl Harbor were just under two years into the unknown future. During this time he trained as an aircraft mechanic, and also as a bombardier. This involved the aiming and releasing of all types of bomb.

Even service life left him restless and bored. Endless training appeared pointless, as it seemed inconceivable that he would ever use it in practice. There was too much spare time. He was single, aimless and out to enjoy himself. He would often be found in clubs, where he drank too much. He wrote later, 'I feel ashamed of events that took place in my life during those years. They did not bring happiness.'[1]

When the Japanese bombed Pearl Harbor without a declaration of war, America was catapulted into a war for which she was largely unprepared. However, the population was united in understandable anger against the aggressor. Most dreamed of revenge.

When a considered response to the bombing of Pearl Harbor was eventually worked out, it needed an exceptional commander. The chosen man was the balding forty-five-year-old Lieutenant Colonel James Doolittle, who was a natural, inspirational leader. Airmen admired him and followed him willingly. He was a superb pilot, totally fearless and with well-grounded technical expertise. Altogether, he was a rare type of man—just the type to lead a dangerous mission.

On DeShazer's base news of the assault on Pearl Harbor was broadcast through loudspeakers. Jake, who had just been reprimanded for a minor offence, was peeling potatoes as a punishment. Hearing the news about Pearl Harbor, he used all his strength to hurl the potatoes at the wall opposite him. It was a natural angry reaction. 'The Japs are going to have to pay for this,' he shouted to the air. And he meant it. There was real hatred in his heart against the Japanese.[2]

At Columbia Air Base, South Carolina, men were told about a dangerous mission and DeShazer, with others, volunteered to train for it. No details of the mission were offered. However, it sounded like a great adventure. Other men who were not involved were noticeably envious of the volunteers. DeShazer enjoyed the excitement of the unknown and the interest and curiosity shown by the other men.

*A B-25 Mitchell bomber preserved at a US air base
in memory of the Doolittle Raid*

The next step was training. At Eglin Air Base in Florida eighty men gathered, including DeShazer. These volunteers were now given initial orders relating to the training. Jake met the other four members of his plane's crew: Lieutenant William Farrow (pilot), Lieutenant Robert Hite (co-pilot), Lieutenant George Barr (navigator) and Sergeant Harold Spatz (engineer/gunner). Corporal Jacob DeShazer was the bombardier.

For a month they practised very short take-offs and low-level flying in their B-25B Mitchell planes. But still nobody except the mission leader, Lieutenant Colonel Doolittle, had any idea what the training was leading up to.

An order came through to fly west across the United States to San Francisco. Once there, the crews of the Mitchells watched, with minds full of unanswered questions, as their planes were hoisted aboard and tied down on to the flight deck of the *Hornet*. Now they realized why short take-offs were so necessary. They were going to have to attempt to take off from the football-pitch length of the carrier's deck. At this point Doolittle urged any man who had doubts or fears about what was to come to drop out and not sail. Nobody responded to his offer.

On 2 April 1942 *Hornet* set sail. DeShazer watched the Golden Gate Bridge above them as they moved out into the Pacific. It was high noon. Everybody on board was excited. Sailors and airmen alike were sharing the sense of adventure. DeShazer recorded: 'I sensed a fighting spirit among the men. We did not need speeches to point out what was wrong with Japan. Every person seemed to know that Japan was an outlaw, and would have to be forced to surrender.'[3]

The loudspeaker system on the *Hornet* informed all the men that the sixteen ships of the task force were heading for Japan. The secret was out. It was America's payback time. The Mitchells were going to bomb Japan.

There was wild cheering at the news. Japan had known nothing but unbroken military success so far. If bombs could be dropped on Japan, it would be a moral victory, a token of the serious revenge to come.

The eighty airmen knew that, even if they could get airborne from the *Hornet's* deck in land-based bombers, there was no question of returning to it. After bombing Japan, they must fly on until they reached China. Much of China was in Japanese hands, so it was a high-risk operation. Could they find a friendly airfield and land? Would they have to bail out when fuel ran out? There were dozens of complicated questions in eighty minds.

5 April 1942 was Easter Day. A solemn Christian service was held on the *Hornet*. Reports emphasize the large number of men who attended. One man who was absent was Jacob DeShazer. To him, prayer and religion were of no interest. The service was irrelevant as far as he was concerned.

At 06.30 on 18 April a Japanese naval vessel spotted the task force and radioed a warning to its headquarters. As a result, the task force itself was now in considerable danger. Admiral Halsey had no option. A message was flashed to *Hornet*: 'Launch planes.'

Doolittle yelled to the men near him, 'Okay, fellas, this is it. Let's go.'[4]

A moment later the blood-chilling klaxon horn sounded its warning. Shipwide loudspeakers blared out: 'Army pilots, man your planes.' The action was starting.

Hornet turned into the twenty-seven-knot wind. With her turbines going flat out, the flight deck pitched and yawed. The waves were thirty feet (nine metres) high. At that moment, Oscar-winning director John Ford captured the scene on film as, one after the other, the sixteen Mitchells took off safely.

DeShazer crouched in the nose of the sixteenth and last aircraft to go, serial number 40–2268. It was 09.20. Somebody had painted 'Bat Out of Hell' on both sides of the plane's nose. Bat's target was Nagoya, about 300 miles south of Tokyo. The flight there seemed endless. On arrival over the target, DeShazer made sure that the bombs were dropped exactly as planned.

As darkness fell, they flew on into China. Fifteen minutes before midnight, the Mitchell ran out of fuel. At about 3,000 feet (a little over 900 metres) somewhere over China, Lieutenant Bill Farrow, the pilot, gave one final order. 'We gotta jump,' he yelled.

DeShazer took to his parachute and floated down. He landed heavily in a Chinese cemetery, fracturing some ribs as he hit the ground.

The total physical damage done by the Doolittle Raid was minimal. However, the boost to American morale was huge. A wave of united rage swept Japan. One of the unexpected results was that their military leaders were lured into the Battle of Midway. This furious air and sea battle marked the beginning of Japan's doom.

None of this helped DeShazer on that April night, however.

He walked for hours, and was eventually taken prisoner by ten Japanese soldiers.

Two American planes had come down in areas of China occupied by the invading Japanese. The sixth Mitchell off *Hornet* crashed into the sea near the Chinese coast. Two of its crew died in the crash. That left eight men in the enemy's hands, five from DeShazer's plane, and three survivors from the crashed plane. These eight men would ultimately be rounded up and sent to Tokyo for questioning. They alone would face the rage of hurt Japanese pride.

Arriving in the Japanese capital, Tokyo, they were taken to a prison run by the Kempeitai. These men were the Japanese military police, not unlike the German Gestapo. The Kempeitai had refined the task of extracting 'confessions' to the point where they knew exactly how far to take a man until he was as near death as possible, yet without killing him completely.

The eight men were held in solitary confinement for forty-six days in Tokyo. All were beaten, kicked, starved, denied sleep, not permitted to wash, shave or remove their uniforms. The wrath of the Japanese nation was focused on them. Finally, DeShazer was shown maps and charts that had been recovered from a wrecked Mitchell. At that point he realized that all the tortures had been needless. Their interrogators already knew the main details of the raid.

The prisoners were now transferred to Bridge House Prison in Shanghai, China, where they spent the next seventy days. Conditions worsened. Lice and rats were everywhere. DeShazer's cell was nine feet long and five feet wide (2.75 metres by 1.5 metres). Dysentery set in. Along with his seven friends, DeShazer was put though a 'show trial' on 28 August 1942. The inevitable verdict was 'Guilty'.

As a result of the mock trial, three of the eight, including DeShazer's pilot, Bill Farrow, and gunner Harold Spatz, were shot on 15 October 1942. DeShazer and four others survived, but did not know the fate of their comrades. However, they were subject to what the kangaroo court called 'special measures'. They were to be treated as criminals, not as prisoners of war. This meant no mail, no Red Cross parcels, no prisoner exchange, inadequate food, solitary confinement, and death if Japan were to lose the war.

Under these conditions, Lieutenant Robert Meder, co-pilot of the sixth plane, died of malnutrition and beriberi on 1 December 1943. He was twenty-six. That left four survivors: Nielsen, the navigator from the sixth plane, DeShazer and two other men from his crew, Barr and Hite. These four prisoners were forced to see Meder's wasted body in a coffin. It depressed them. Hopelessness set in. DeShazer was struggling to stay sane while fighting loneliness and uncertainty. As he wrote later, it was coupled with a 'hatred for the Japanese people that nearly drove me crazy'.[5]

While DeShazer was enduring the intolerable, one raider who had returned to America, Ted Lawson, dictated to a writer the story of the Doolittle Raid and his part in it. The press rushed out the book called *Thirty Seconds over Tokyo*. It was dedicated to the eight missing men, now presumed dead. One of the eight names on the book's dedication page is, of course, that of Jacob DeShazer. Hollywood immediately showed interest in filming the story. With official permission, an accurate film with the same title appeared in 1944. The scenes of the planes taking off from *Hornet* are the actual film footage taken on 18 April 1942 by director John Ford. The film was a huge success at the time, and remains a respectable tribute to the raiders.

After Lieutenant Meder's death, it was obvious that no raider would survive unless conditions improved. News of his death reached the Nanking military headquarters. The prison commanding officer made an appearance and asked the prisoners what they would like to eat. DeShazer came to believe that the Japanese top brass knew that they were very likely to lose the war, and were worried about American retaliation if any more raiders died. Whatever the truth of this, conditions improved slightly. A few books, including a Bible, were brought for them to read. The prisoners found out that the books had been looted from the former home of a missionary to China.

None of the four was religious, but each read the Bible, and for each man it provided a message that linked them back to sanity. Bob Hite, the co-pilot, wrote, 'It was the first time any of us had really read the Bible from cover to cover.' Hite began to feel sorrow instead of hatred for the Japanese guards. For all of them, 'The words took on a deep meaning and conveyed a new hope for their future.'[6]

One day DeShazer was cleaning his cell when a guard looked in and yelled, 'Hayaku!' ('Hurry up!'). DeShazer had been festering with rage. He yelled back, 'Go jump in the lake.' Later he recorded: 'Before I knew what was going to happen, the door was unlocked, and the guard hit me on the head with his fist. I immediately kicked him in the stomach with my bare foot, and he hit me with his steel scabbard. I had been using some water on the floor to mop up my cell. I picked up the dirty mop water and threw it on the guard. It cooled him off enough so that he didn't do any more than swear at me. But it is strange that he didn't cut off my head.'[7] There is no doubt that DeShazer was fortunate not to be killed as a result of the incident. Other men were killed for less.

In May 1944 his turn came to read the Bible. The guard told him he could have it for three weeks. It proved to be an experience that turned his life upside down. The only light in the solitary cell came through the vent at the top of one wall. It was enough. In the leaflet *I Was a Prisoner of Japan* DeShazer outlined what happened:

I eagerly began to read its pages. Chapter after chapter gripped my heart. In due time I came to the books of the prophets, and found that their every writing seemed focused on a divine Redeemer from sin, one who was to be sent from heaven to be born in the form of a human babe. Their writings so fascinated me that I read them again and again until I had earnestly studied them through six times. Then I went on into the New Testament, and there read of the birth of Jesus Christ, the one who actually fulfilled the very prophecies of Isaiah, Jeremiah, Micah and the other Old Testament writers. My heart rejoiced as I found confirmed in Acts 10:43: 'To him give all the prophets witness, that through his name, whosoever believeth on him shall receive remission [forgiveness] of sins.' After I had carefully read this book of the Acts, I continued on into the study of the epistle Paul wrote to the Christians at Rome.

On June 8th, 1944, the words of Romans 10:9 stood out boldly before my eyes: 'If thou shalt confess with thy mouth the Lord Jesus, and shalt believe in thine heart that God raised him from the dead, thou shalt be saved.' In that very moment God gave me grace to confess my sins to him, and he forgave me and saved me for Jesus' sake, even as I later found that His Word ... promises so clearly in 1 John 1:9: 'If we confess our sins, [God] is faithful and just to forgive us our sins, and to cleanse us from all unrighteousness.'

How my heart rejoiced in my newness of spiritual life, even though my body was suffering so terribly from the physical beatings and lack of food. But suddenly I discovered that God had given me new spiritual eyes, and that when I looked at the Japanese officers and guards who had starved and beaten me and my companions so cruelly, I found my bitter hatred for them changed to loving pity ... I read in my Bible that while those who crucified Jesus on the cross had beaten him and spit upon him before he was nailed to the cross, he tenderly prayed in his moment of excruciating suffering, 'Father, forgive them for they know not what they do.' And now from the depths of my heart, I too prayed for God to forgive my torturers ...

DeShazer's new faith in God was soon tested. Going to a cell to clean a toilet, he was escorted by a guard who was in a hurry. This man pushed and slapped him on the back while yelling, 'Hayaku! Hayaku!' Before DeShazer was in the cell, the guard slammed the door, trapping his prisoner's foot. Instead of opening the door to release it, he began kicking the trapped bare foot with hobnailed boots. Eventually DeShazer was able to wrench himself free. 'The pain in my foot was severe, and I thought some bones were broken. I felt as if God were testing me somehow.'[8]

When the guard came on duty the next morning, DeShazer seriously considered revenge. Then he remembered the Bible, and instead he called out, 'Ohayo gozaimasu!' ('Good morning'). The guard gave him a strange look. Every morning DeShazer tried the same friendly greeting. One day the guard spoke to him through the door. They talked to each other. Then the guard became friendly and from that time on did not shout at him or treat him rudely. On one occasion, he opened the little observation door and handed DeShazer a boiled sweet potato. Another time DeShazer received five figs. He wrote later, 'I knew then that God's way will work if we really try, no matter what the circumstances.'[9]

The fact that Jacob DeShazer was so evidently spiritually changed and renewed did not help his poor physical condition. By June 1944 twenty-six months of solitary imprisonment, bad treatment and inadequate food had taken a terrible toll of the four raiders in the enemy's hands. All had to live through a further year of imprisonment in Nanking.

On 15 June 1945 DeShazer and his three friends were hurriedly transferred by train to prison in Peking (Beijing). The hard men of the Kempeitai ran it. Every night they could hear the torture and screams of the other captives. After a month of further ill treatment, the emaciated DeShazer, weakened by attacks of dysentery, developed huge boils all over his body, even under his feet. In his boredom, he decided to count the boils. He reached seventy-five and gave up. There were more. His hands could not reach between his shoulders. Worse still, his heart was hurting and he recalled that Lieutenant Meder had spoken of his heart being painful just before he died. 'I thought that I would probably die for the same reason,' he remembered.[10] As DeShazer was becoming delirious, the navigator of 'Bat out of Hell', the red-headed Lieutenant George Barr, lost the use of his mind. All four surviving raiders were nearing death.

Shortly afterwards a medical orderly came to DeShazer's cell and gave him a vitamin injection. Somebody in the Japanese hierarchy must have decided to try to keep the men alive. From this point onwards, they were given regular meals of good food.

It was 9 August 1945. DeShazer suddenly felt compelled to pray for peace. He attributed this to the Holy Spirit. After some hours he felt that God was insistently telling him that he was to stop praying in this way because victory had been won. He had no radio or any means of knowing that this was the exact day that the final atomic bomb was dropped on Nagasaki. Within days the majority in the Japanese government wanted peace. Unconditional surrender followed. The Second World War was over.

Though still in prison, DeShazer was gaining some vitality. Parallel with the better treatment came an experience of the love of God such as is given to few people. He wrote, 'I felt the love of God flooding my soul. Night and day I experienced joy. I felt sure I was having a foretaste of heaven … Jesus was as real and alive to me as anyone could possibly be.'[11]

Even before he was released he felt called to be a Christian missionary to the Japanese people. The very idea frightened him. He had no talents or skills as a public speaker. He lacked theological college training. At the same time, he knew that he had promised that he would do God's will. He intended to keep that promise.

Finally, on 20 August 1945 the cell doors were opened. DeShazer and the other three surviving raiders were free. Forty months of incessant suffering were over.

For the first time the world learned the fate of two of Doolittle's Mitchell crews that had gone down in enemy-controlled China on 18 April 1942. Eight men had been captured. Four had paid the supreme penalty. The remaining four, sustained by faith and fortitude, had barely survived to tell their stories.

Back home in America at Salem, Oregon, was a praying mother. Mrs Hulda Andrus had prayed earnestly for her lost son for forty months. Now the news release that she heard on the radio reported that four missing Doolittle raiders had been found alive. No names were given. Would her son be one of the four? Helen Andrus, Jake's half-sister, could hardly move away from her radio. At noon on Monday, 20 August 1945, the news came through: one of the four men was 'Sergeant' Jacob DeShazer. When he asked about the promotion from corporal, he was told that he became a sergeant the moment the wheels of his Mitchell lifted from the *Hornet's* deck!

Ahead of DeShazer lay the homecoming, a period in hospital and the recovery of his health and weight. When he was feeling better, he started to respond to the press, who naturally wanted to learn the details of his story, particularly his imprisonment. This brought out the changes in his spiritual outlook. Newspapermen seemed fascinated by his desire to go back to Japan. Press opinion was unanimous that he was sincere, but almost all agreed that the

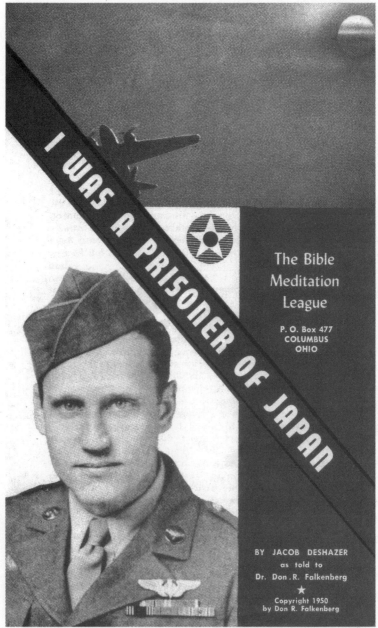

Front cover of a tract written by Jacob DeShazer. It was the Japanese translation of this which proved so influential in the life of Mitsuo Fuchida.

plan would be short-lived. At a human level it was probably a reasonable point of view.

DeShazer had committed himself to the Free Methodist Church. Invitations to tell his story and answer questions about his conversion and new life in Christ came from many quarters. At one church he was asked if he had ever been baptized. He responded that he had been baptized. He recalled that while he was in prison, he had wished that he could be baptized. He also recalled that at that time he had actually gone over to one side of his prison cell where the wind was blowing water from the eaves through the window. He stood in this spattering rain and praised God for a water baptism in the name of the Father, Son and the Holy Spirit.

After some time of recuperation, he enrolled at Seattle Pacific College to prepare himself for missionary work in Japan. It was at this college in 1946 that he met and married his wife Florence, who proved to be an ideal support to him. Together, they sailed for Japan in 1948, just six years and eight months after he had set out to fly to Japan with a very different purpose. They eventually had five children, some born in Japan.

DeShazer wrote a very simplified account of the Doolittle Raid, what happened to the eight men who fell into Japanese hands and how he had been transformed by the message of the Bible. Many millions of copies in leaflet form were printed in Japanese and widely

Jacob DeShazer in later life

distributed in the immediate post-war years. By any standards, it is an impressive story.

It was a copy of this leaflet that was given to the forty-seven-year-old Mitsuo Fuchida at Shibuya railway station in Tokyo in 1950. As we saw in the previous chapter, Fuchida had been the leader of the attack on Pearl Harbor in December 1941. After Japan's defeat, Fuchida's life lacked direction and purpose. He was in Tokyo to testify at war crimes trials against some of the top wartime Japanese leaders. Reading the leaflet *I Was a Prisoner of Japan* by Jacob DeShazer influenced him greatly. Fuchida bought a Bible and read it. He realized that no amount of good deeds would put him right with God. All he had to offer God was sin and evil. By April 1950 he experienced forgiveness of sins, spiritual renewal and had a personal faith in Christ. There and then he dedicated the remainder of his life to serving the Lord who had saved him.

Mitsuo Fuchida and Jacob DeShazer, once on opposite sides in a bitter war, were now united together by a common faith in Christ. Photographs of the former enemies now sharing a profound friendship are deeply moving. They remained friends and colleagues until Fuchida died. DeShazer attended his funeral, and told everybody who asked that it was basically a joyous occasion, because his friend had gone to heaven.

The DeShazers gave thirty years of their lives to Japan. They were even responsible for planting a Christian church in Nagoya, the place bombed by Jake in the Doolittle Raid. One high spot in his ministry came when Captain Kato became a Christian. He was the guard who had given the prisoners a Bible in the Nanking prison. One couple who came to Christian faith when Rev. Jake DeShazer, the Free Methodist missionary, preached in their village served as missionaries for many years in Brazil.

Everything DeShazer did in Japan had the unanimous support of the surviving raiders. They even backed him financially. In turn, DeShazer tried never to miss a reunion. The DeShazer story still continues. It lives on in the Japanese people who found faith in Christ because of him. It certainly lives on in accounts of the Doolittle Raid and the story of his resulting imprisonment.

DeShazer died in March 2008. Although his silver goblet is now turned upside down, his story lives on.

More information on Jacob DeShazer

After the war, the first Christian publication that DeShazer wrote was the tract *I Was a Prisoner of Japan* (Bible Meditation League, 1950). The League followed it with *I am the Praying Mother of Jacob DeShazer* by Mrs Hulda Andrus.

There are several other writings, including *DeShazer Returns* (Free Methodist World Headquarters, 1970), '30 Years After Tokyo' (*Decision* magazine, April 1972), 'How Can a POW Love his Enemy?' (*Freeway* magazine, 7 April 1974). C. Hoyt Watson, the principal of Seattle Pacific College, wrote a book in 1950 called *The Amazing Story of Sergeant Jacob DeShazer*. Galaxy Communications revised this with an epilogue by Leona Fear in 1991. A recent leaflet by Bible Literature International called *Finding Forgiveness at Pearl Harbor* is worth looking at.

In the US the Doolittle Raid is almost as well known as Pearl Harbor. There are a lot of relevant books. *The Doolittle Raid* by Carroll V. Glines (1988) is a particularly good account of the raid.

The author's own correspondence with DeShazer began in the 1970s. At first the story was used in schools to interest youngsters in their Religious Education lessons. Jacob

DeShazer was delighted that his testimony was written up so that others could be blessed and encouraged by reading it. He checked it for accuracy and supplied photographs, booklets and information to promote the use of the story.

8

Ernest Gordon

Author of Miracle on the River Kwai

Work on the railway commenced every day at dawn and ended at dusk. The men worked in pitiless heat, seven days a week without breaks. Wearing next to nothing, they were beaten and tortured. The small amount of rice that formed their staple diet reduced men to mere skin-wrapped skeletons.

Ernest Gordon while president of CREED

8

Ernest Gordon[1]

In a quiet part of western Thailand, seventy-three miles from Bangkok, lies a beautiful place called Chungkai on the banks of the River Kwai. It is little known to most of the Thai people, but to Ernest Gordon it is a place never to be forgotten.

Today a beautiful garden cemetery remains in the exact place where Ernest Gordon was once a prisoner of war (see overleaf). The gardeners work under the mango trees and among the long rows of stones that mark the graves of many young men who lie buried there. In that sad and isolated place, only the songs of the birds break the silence. Yet, from Chungkai, Ernest Gordon brought a story of spiritual triumph which still sounds out around the world.

Born at Greenock in 1916, Ernest Gordon grew up with his brother Pete and sister Grace in lighthouses on the west coast of Scotland. Theirs was not a rich family, but it was united and friendly. When Ernest was six he could already sail and fish. Every month his father bought him a book. At fifteen he went to sea as an apprentice in the Merchant Navy, but after ten months his

159

The cemetery at Chungkai

ship was taken out of service as a result of the severe economic
depression that badly affected Britain in the interwar years. As a
result, he returned to school, Greenock Academy, and from there
progressed to Glasgow University for two years. The costs were
high, so he decided he ought to earn enough money to finish his
studies.

To achieve this, he was commissioned as a pilot in the Royal
Air Force. In the course of a flight in a Hart biplane from a
training school, some faulty equipment caused a crash near
Bishop's Stortford. His skull was fractured and his spine damaged.
Although recovered, he was given non-flying duties. Unhappy at
being prevented from flying, he went to St Andrew's University in
1937, using a small disability payment from the RAF to defray the
financial burden.

Besides studying history and philosophy, he enjoyed outdoor
pursuits. In his early twenties Ernest Gordon enjoyed all that life
had to offer. At six feet two inches tall (1.88 m.) and weighing

over 200 pounds (over ninety kilos), he was an impressive figure. He was a light-heavyweight boxer and a keen rugby player. In vacations he raced for Britain in international yacht races. Always at ease in the company of tough, aggressive men, he enjoyed adventure. As might be expected, he was an optimist who believed only in the power of human reason to solve the problems of the world. There was no place in his thinking for spiritual matters.

The drums of war were sounding louder. His attitude was that if he could not fight in the air then he would fight on the ground. He did not wait to be drafted into the army, but volunteered before the war started and was soon commissioned as an officer in the Argyll and Sutherland Highlanders. By March 1941 he was a captain in charge of 'A' Company in the 2nd Battalion of the 93rd Highlanders in Malaya. Their orders were to defend Malaya in the event of an attack by Hitler's allies, the Japanese.

Japan was indeed planning to attack Malaya. Its first action had been to start the Second World War in the Pacific by bombing the American battleships anchored in Pearl Harbor. The day following that action, 8 December 1941, two well-prepared Japanese divisions landed in northern Malaya with the intention of driving the defending British forces down to Singapore Island, 350 miles to the south.

During the fighting for Malaya, Captain Gordon was wounded twice, once by machine-gun bullets in his shoulder. There were 1,000 men in his battalion, but by the time they had been forced back through the jungle to Singapore, only 120 were left. The battle for Singapore Island reduced them to thirty men. In fifty-eight days the Japanese had triumphed and over 80,000 British and Commonwealth troops were made prisoners of war.

Never a man to give in easily, Gordon attempted to avoid capture. He and nine friends got together and bought a small boat for 2,000 dollars. The aim was to sail it across the Indian Ocean to the safety of Ceylon (now Sri Lanka). Half the journey had been completed when a Japanese ship stopped them. Bearded and barefoot, the disappointed men were taken to join thousands of other captives at Singapore.

So began three and a half years as a prisoner of war. In the camp at Changi, he realized that the stories about Japanese cruelties were true. For instance, one of the first Japanese atrocities was to go through the Alexandra Hospital in Singapore and bayonet to

Ernest Gordon photographed in Singapore in 1942 before capture

death all the helpless patients, nurses and doctors. Plainly, they had no intention of keeping the civilized rules of the Geneva Conventions governing the treatment of prisoners of war. As a result, Ernest Gordon correctly described those three and a half years as a period of 'unspeakable horror'.

He had not been a prisoner very long when he needed an operation for appendicitis. A doctor, who was also a prisoner, laid the patient on a kitchen table and performed the surgery successfully. Being a strong man, he soon recovered.

The spirits of the prisoners at Changi were so low that many looked for help in religion. The Japanese allowed church services, most of which took place out of doors. Men prayed in fear, not faith. They prayed for food and they prayed to be spared death.

Ernest Gordon would not attend services for the wrong reason. As he saw it, these men were turning to religion as an insurance against suffering.

Some Christian prisoners were not much help either. Influenced by the churches they had come from and as a result of holding mistaken views about biblical prophecy, they made things worse by going round quoting verses from Daniel and Revelation. They claimed that these verses proved that the war would soon be over. How tragically wrong they were!

At this point, Ernest Gordon was about to be linked to one of the best-known stories of this terrible war. Orders came that he and thousands of others were to move out of Changi by rail to Banpong. Packed in metal freight wagons, they were to be used as slave labour.

The Japanese high command planned to attack India. To assist their plans, they proposed to build a railway 258 miles long through the jungles of Thailand and Burma. Their engineers reckoned it would take five or six years, but with thousands of slave labourers the task could be speeded up.

Beginning in October 1942, work on the railway commenced every day at dawn and ended at dusk. The men worked in pitiless heat, seven days a week without breaks. Wearing next to nothing, they were beaten and tortured. The small amount of rice that formed their staple diet reduced men to mere skin-wrapped skeletons. The Japanese gave them no medical attention. To them, human life was cheap, especially the life of a soldier who had surrendered.

Ernest Gordon was at the base camp of Chungkai. The prisoners made their own bamboo huts, which had 'floors' inside, effectively raising their sleeping quarters just above the mud. The roofs were made of palm leaves. Each man had an area to himself that was six feet by two feet (180 by 60 cm.), the size of a narrow grave.

In the spring of 1943 the guards were told that the work was not going fast enough. So men were beaten without mercy. Many men fell to the ground and died with the words 'Speedo, Speedo' being the final sounds they heard on this earth. In this way the guards added to the grim harvest of death. If a guard thought a man was disobedient, the most horrible, sadistic and disgusting tortures were carried out. In every way it was 'a death railway'.

In addition to beating and torture, men died of disease. The bodies of cholera victims had to be burnt. Gordon looked at the blazing pyres and saw men placed on them who had once been friends, husbands and sons. Death was calling from every direction.

The bridge over the River Kwai was built in early 1943. It was a minor part of the railway project that was made famous by a post-war film. Although Ernest Gordon did not work on the bridge, he wrote forcefully against the film. All survivors agree that the film may be entertaining, but it is total fiction. The fiction is that British prisoners built it willingly to show their efficiency. The fact is that they built it at bayonet point. The prisoners continually looked for ways to sabotage the bridge, which they fiercely hated.

Things became so bad throughout the length of the railway that the prisoners at Chungkai and elsewhere became selfish. Men called out as they lay dying and others who were passing by turned their heads away. Sometimes the sick were ignored. Prisoners even stole from one another and fought over scraps of food. Some robbed the dead. Hatred of the Japanese kept some going. Though for many morality vanished and morale hit rock bottom, there were always a few who kept faith and integrity. Cursing became an obsession. Some could make up sentences in which every word was a curse. A few cursed God.

'Death House'—that is what the helpless prisoners called the hut that served as Chungkai 'hospital'. Ernest Gordon was moved there because diphtheria robbed him of the ability to walk. He had kept on his feet with malaria, dysentery and beriberi. He had become so thin that he could encircle his thigh with the fingers of his hand. Now he was on his back and incapable of feeling hunger or pain. That was a bad sign. He overheard a doctor say, 'The only thing left is to let him have a decent end.'

The floor of the 'hospital' was a sea of mud. The smell of overflowing latrines and rotting bodies was terrible. Flies swarmed over all the patients. Gordon pleaded to be moved to the morgue simply because it was cleaner. His companions there were dead men wrapped in rice sacks. He wrote a last letter to his parents and settled down to await the end.

However, some of his friends who were Christians had other ideas. They moved him to an outhouse under the eaves of a hut. Dusty Miller washed the pus out of his leg ulcers and, with Dinty Moore, another friend, began nursing him. Dusty, Dinty and Tom Rigden believed, for some reason, that Gordon was worth saving. If he survived perhaps he would be the sort of man who could do something to make a better world after the war was over. He described his three would-be rescuers as 'rare characters'. All of them were motivated by deep faith and genuine human kindliness. They were very different, yet alike in being 'nature's gentlemen'.

Only in 1965, twenty-three years after the event, did Ernest Gordon find out that his friend Tom Rigden had sold his precious Rolex watch in order to procure some emetine, the cure for amoebic dysentery. Without it, Gordon would have been dead within two weeks. At the time, Tom said nothing. Remarkably, after a few weeks of this 'nursing', Gordon could hobble with the aid of a stick. Although he was still affected with many illnesses, the fact that just one was cured enabled him to struggle back from the brink of death.

On his twenty-seventh birthday in May 1943, the friends who saved him from death made him a birthday cake from rice, limes, bananas and palm sugar. Gordon wrote, 'I have had tastier birthday cakes in my life, but none which meant so much to me.'

It was about this time that the miracle on the River Kwai happened at Chungkai.

First, there was a series of incidents involving Christians. One soldier, Angus McGillivray, was determined to save his best friend when he became ill. Over a period of time, he gave all his own food rations to his friend without telling him of the sacrifice he was making. The sick man recovered. Then one day Angus fell down and died of starvation. Dusty Miller remarked to Ernest Gordon that the incident reminded him of this passage from the Bible: 'My command is this: Love each other as I have loved you. Greater love has no one than this, that he lay down his life for his friends' (John 15:13).

They heard of an Australian soldier who was caught outside the camp trying to obtain medicine from the local Thais for sick friends. The Japanese sentenced him to death for this and insisted that all the men in the camp were to watch his execution. The Australian calmly knelt down, drew a New Testament from his ragged shorts, and read from it. He then put the book away, smiled and called out: 'Cheer up; it isn't as bad as all that. I'll be all right.' He knelt, bent his head forward, and a Samurai sword flashed in the sunlight as he was killed.

On another occasion, at the end of a day's work, a guard declared that a shovel was missing. Working himself up into an uncontrollable rage, he screamed: 'All die! All die!'

Just as the guard was about to begin shooting the whole group, one man stepped forward and said, 'I did it.' Seizing the rifle by the barrel, the guard brought it down on the prisoner's head. The Scottish soldier sank to the ground, dead. When the shovels were counted afterwards, they were all there. The guard had simply made a mistake.

Such acts of self-sacrifice made other prisoners ask, 'Is there anything in Christianity?' A new spirit of thinking about others became more evident in the camp.

Ernest Gordon was not convinced that the Bible was true. He argued against Dusty's faith. Didn't Dusty realize that twenty young men were dying in Chungkai every day? 'Why doesn't God do something, instead of just sitting on his big, white throne in heaven?' Gordon asked.

Dusty thought for a moment and replied, 'We can't see everything God is doing now. I suppose one day we'll see and then we'll understand.'

At this time there was an incident outside the camp that influenced Ernest Gordon. Quite frequently as the prisoners tramped through local Thai villages on the way to work, they encountered yellow-robed Buddhist priests with their silver begging bowls. Buddhism was, and still is, the dominant religion in Thailand. The philosophy of the priests was non-attachment to the world. Thus, if a prisoner dropped at the side of the road and was obviously dying, they would ignore him. The pitiful condition of the slave labourers was of no concern to them. There was no place for mercy in their thinking.

One day the wretched prisoners passed through a village where the inhabitants, at some risk to themselves, gave them food, medicine and money. On enquiry, it was discovered that through the influence of a missionary, the villagers had been converted from Buddhism to Christianity. The contrast between the ethics of Buddhism and Christianity were crystal clear to the observant prisoners. Again, the question asked itself: was there more to what the Bible taught than Ernest Gordon had thought?

His questioning was still going on when an Australian sergeant dropped in one evening. The two men had never met before. The visitor wanted Gordon to lead a discussion group with the object of finding out what the Bible taught and if it was true. 'My men think you are right for the job because you are a fighting soldier and you've been to university,' he was told.

They did not want 'Sunday School stuff'. They wanted 'the real thing'—strictly no 'waffling', which was the gentle art of avoiding the facts. The question to be answered was: 'What did Jesus really teach?' How could these teachings have anything to do with their lives?

Feeling very unsure of himself, Gordon read from a Bible another prisoner had given him. They gathered in a bamboo grove near the 'hospital'. He reported what the Gospels taught to the discussion group next evening. At each successive meeting, numbers grew. Men knew that unaided human reason had nothing to offer them. Why not look elsewhere?

Ernest Gordon and his friends gradually came to know Jesus as a real person in their lives. The cross showed that God, through Jesus, knew all about suffering. There was no obvious explanation, other than sin, to explain why people suffered, but at least they came to believe that God cared. At that time, their biggest question was: 'How do I face death?' To that, human reason offers poor answers, or no answer at all. But Jesus said, 'I am the resurrection and the life. He who believes in me will live, even though he dies; and whoever lives and believes in me will never die' (John 11:25–26). These men, including Gordon, approached God through Jesus. Some died trusting in Christ and listening to the Word of God. They knew that God was with them as they neared the end of their lives.

It was there at Chungkai in 1943 that Ernest Gordon and many others became real Christians. They experienced the new life of the Holy Spirit within them, enabling them to believe in Christ, who had died for them and was gloriously raised again. As a result, a church came into being—not a building, but men united by faith in Jesus as Lord and Saviour. They held worship services. They prayed. For bread and wine they had rice and rice water. There was even a Bible-lending library. A man could borrow a Bible for one hour at a time.

This church without walls had all the marks of the biblical

model, including an evangelistic spirit. Some British soldiers found two Chinese still alive after a massacre perpetrated by the Japanese. The two men were equipped with fictitious identities and absorbed into the life of Chungkai camp. Christians witnessed to them. They were converted. There in the camp they were baptized and admitted into the church without walls.

On Christmas Day 1943, over 2,000 men attended a service. It was a better Christmas when compared with 1942. There was a new spirit everywhere at Chungkai. Stealing from the living and the dead ceased. Men really cared about one another. Although the guards were as brutal as ever, it seemed to many men that a miracle had happened. Those whose sickness was less intense gave blood for the more seriously ill. They respected the dead and buried them carefully. Chungkai was transformed by numerous acts of faith and sacrificial love. Ernest Gordon knew that if he survived, he would take his newly found faith into the post-war world.

The death railway had been completed in the autumn of 1943, but the suffering and dying went on in all camps across the Japanese Empire until the aggressors were finally crushed.

Good Friday 1945 was important. That was the day Ernest Gordon was finally able to forgive the Japanese. They did not deserve forgiveness. The guards and their masters knew perfectly well that what they had done was evil. Nevertheless, the Christian has to pray, 'Forgive us our sins, for we also forgive everyone who sins against us' (Luke 11:4). And did not Christ on the cross pray, 'Father, forgive them for they do not know what they are doing'? (Luke 23:24).

The test came when a train moved Ernest Gordon and some fellow Chungkai prisoners towards Bangkok. They were shunted into a siding alongside some trucks loaded with desperately wounded Japanese troops. These men, the refuse of war, were ignored by their own side and waited fatalistically for death.

Without a word, Ernest Gordon and some fellow officers went
to give them water. Both the Japanese guards and other British
soldiers preferred to let them die. 'You are fools. They are the
enemy,' one man protested. Eighteen months earlier these men
from Chungkai would gladly have murdered any Japanese had it
been possible. Having read the Bible, they recalled the story of the
Good Samaritan. Now they obeyed its teaching. Many a time in
later life Ernest Gordon reflected that it was right to forgive and
not allow bitterness to dominate his life.

15 August 1945 was the day the war in the Pacific ended and
freedom came. With a friend he gazed across the hills towards
Chungkai and recited in full the lovely words of Psalm 121 which
begins:

I lift up my eyes to the hills—
    where does my help come from?
My help comes from the LORD,
    the Maker of heaven and earth ...

Soon afterwards he learned that Dusty Miller, one of the
Christians who had helped to save his life when he was in 'Death
House', had been crucified by being nailed to a tree just before the
end of the war. Tears clouded his eyes. Dusty's 'crime' was simply
being an unbreakable Christian. The waste of young life like this
made Gordon determined to spend the rest of his life working
amongst young people.

Back home in Scotland it took months in hospital to recover
from malaria, hepatitis and ulcerated intestines. Helen Robertson
became his wife, and Alastair and Gillian were born soon
afterwards. In 1950 he was ordained as a Church of Scotland
minister and worked for three years in Paisley. He was then pastor
of Presbyterian churches at Amagansett and Montauk in the US,
where he is remembered 'for his eloquent preaching and kind

heart'. In 1955 he received an invitation to be dean of the chapel at Princeton University, America. He had finally achieved his ambition to work amongst young people.

When the present writer asked about the Princeton years, Gordon wrote in a letter, 'I study the Bible every day. I find there is always something to learn which guides me in my work. This work is being minister to 3,500 undergraduates, 1,500 graduate students plus 1,000 in faculty and administration. What often counts most in my work of preaching, teaching, and counselling is the friendships I form, usually through being there to help someone overcome a problem. I am constantly surprised by the grace of God at work in the lives of people I know.' He wrote a book called *Meet me at the Door*, which describes the work in detail.

Retirement from Princeton came in 1981. He filled his retirement by being the founder and very active president of CREED. The acronym means 'Christian Rescue Effort for the Emancipation of Dissidents'. CREED did all in its power to secure the release of those unjustly imprisoned for their faith. He travelled widely and used the influence of powerful people in successive American governments either to gain freedom for prisoners, or at least to send them help and encouragement. The activities of CREED would fill a book.

Although Dr Ernest Gordon wrote several other books, none has equalled the status of one of the greatest spiritual classics, *Miracle on the River Kwai*. That great work has appeared with various titles since 1963. In 2002 it was reissued as *To End All Wars*, to coincide with an American film with the same title that purports to tell his story. As with many such films on historical themes, the truth is distorted and lost.

Miracle on the River Kwai includes these words: 'I know the depths to which men could sink and the heights to which they could rise. I could speak from experience of despair, but also of hope; of hatred, but also of love; of man without God, but also of man sustained by God. God in Christ has shared man's suffering … even that experience which seems to defeat us all, namely, death.' The book ends with the memorable sentence: 'He comes into our Death House to lead us through it.'

So Ernest Gordon not only survived the death camps of the River Kwai. He also found the living God there and kept his vow to spend the rest of his life in a useful way—proclaiming the gospel of the grace of God, and helping those unjustly imprisoned.

In January 2002, at the age of eighty-five, Ernest Gordon died at Princeton, USA. (Helen, his wife for fifty-one years, died in 1997.) He had been an airman, a tough soldier, a tortured prisoner, a husband, a father, a Christian minister, a scholar, a campaigner for those unjustly imprisoned, a man who led a full life, yet at heart he was a man with a simple trust in the personal God he came to know on the banks of the River Kwai.

More information on Ernest Gordon

Much of the detail in this story comes from personal correspondence, which started in 1972. The *Reader's Digest* article 'It Happened on the River Kwai' (June 1960) is worth consulting. I have a complete set of the CREED literature and have referred to it regularly. Ernest Gordon's son, Alastair, sent me a copy of his *Eulogy for My Father*, which I found very moving. It has details not found in his father's books. The obituaries from *The New York Times* (20 January 2002), *The Scotsman* (9 January 2002) and *The Presbyterian Outlook* (24 January 2002) all add small details to the story in *Miracle on the River Kwai*, which stands on its own as a moving Christian classic.

9

Rupert Lonsdale

Captain of HM Submarine *Seal*

> '*Dear God,*' *he prayed,* '*we have tried everything in our power to save ourselves and we have failed. Yet we believe that you can do things that are impossible to men. Please, O Lord, deliver us.*' ...

> *The answer to their prayers came almost immediately.*

Rupert Lonsdale

9

Rupert Lonsdale

I n the early hours of 5 May 1940 Lieutenant Commander Rupert Lonsdale's submarine seemed doomed to be stuck for ever on the sea floor.

Then a series of events occurred that resulted in what most of the crew thought was a miracle. The submarine broke loose from the mud of the seabed and managed to surface. The crew's rejoicing that they would not die trapped under the sea was stifled by the realization that HMS/M *Seal* was like a stranded whale. It could not dive for cover. It could not move to evade attack. It would only be a short time before the enemy came hunting their prey. And they did.

Sure enough, German bombs and bullets reduced the submarine to battered helplessness. Once its two Lewis machine guns had seized up there was no way to fight back. Surrender was the only option. A German Arado 196 seaplane landed nearby. With its guns pointing at the helpless men, a German officer demanded to know who was the captain. Lonsdale waved his hand. 'Swim over to my plane,' ordered the German. Having handed over control of his submarine and crew to his second in command, Lonsdale

An Arado 196—the type of German seaplane which first attacked Seal and then landed on the sea to receive Lonsdale's surrender

dived into the water. He surrendered and was taken prisoner. The German plane lifted from the sea with its important captive.

The first day of captivity was his thirty-fifth birthday. It was not a birthday that he was ever likely to forget. As he was flown away, he could not stop himself reflecting about how his men would be treated. His life from now on would be long and eventful, but it is not really understandable without knowing what preceded the events of that nerve-racking day in May 1940.

Lonsdale's father was a civil servant who had worked for most of his life in Nigeria. After education at St Cyprian's School, Eastbourne, Rupert Lonsdale decided to join the Royal Navy as a cadet in 1919. This involved spending four years at two Royal Navy colleges, Osborne and Dartmouth. After serving in the light cruiser HMS *Carysfoot* and the battleship HMS *Ramillies*, he volunteered for the submarine service in 1927, when he was twenty-two.

Within four years he was promoted to be first lieutenant, or second in command, of several different types of submarine. In 1934 he passed the course for prospective submarine commanders.

The test was so difficult that it was known as 'the Perisher'. An officer being tested had to pass first time. Second attempts were not allowed.

Also in 1934 he was given his first command, a small submarine of 440 tons (15,400 cubic feet, or 436 cubic metres) called *H.44*, a leftover from the First World War. His second command, for one year in 1937, was a newer boat called *Swordfish* (all submarines are referred to as 'boats'). The following year Lieutenant Commander Lonsdale was appointed as captain of *Seal*. This boat, built at Chatham, was the last of a group of six designed primarily as minelayers.

Rupert Lonsdale's Christian faith deepened throughout his career in the Royal Navy. His experience never included a Damascus Road 'crisis' like that of the

Rupert Lonsdale in 1935

apostle Paul. Both his parents were Christians, but he knew that he had to believe in Christ for himself. By his teenage years the matter was settled. His personal relationship with God was based on repentance and faith in Christ as his Saviour and Lord. He was sure that Christ was the Son of God and that through his cross and resurrection he now had eternal life. He often said that in difficult times as an officer in submarines he prayed and always received help. In fact, so many times had his prayers been answered that he found it hard *not* to believe in God and his grace.

1939 was a year full of rumours about another war. In the early months of that year, the crew assembled and met their commanding officer. Rupert Lonsdale did not fit the image of the typical submarine commander, swashbuckling and hard-drinking. He was clean-shaven, slim, of medium height, a quiet man, but firm in decision.

Every one of the fifty-nine men in the crew knew three things about him. The first was that he had a fine record as a successful submarine commander. The second was that his wife had died a year or so previously in giving birth to his only child, a son called John. The third affirmed that he was a good-living man with no wild ways. Some had noticed a well-used Bible in their captain's cabin. Most of them worked out quickly that he was a committed Christian. It was obvious that he took the Bible seriously. The men wondered what difference that would make to the way he controlled both his submarine and his crew.

Sunday, 3 September 1939, found *Seal* operating near Aden. In a formal way the entire crew was lined up on the metal casing. Lonsdale read out a signal from the Admiralty. Without fuss or comment, they were told what they had all expected for some time: Britain, the Royal Navy and *Seal* were at war with Hitler's Germany.

Having returned to home waters, *Seal* carried out several dangerous war patrols. In one, Lonsdale was 'mentioned in dispatches', which is the Royal Navy's way of giving praise for bravery and skill. Then in April 1940 Admiral Max Horton, the officer in charge of all British submarines, devised Operation FD7 for *Seal*. This was to enter the Skagerrak, the stretch of water between the north of Denmark and Norway, and proceed to the more dangerous Kattegat, between the east of Denmark and Sweden (leading to northern Germany). *Seal* was to lay her fifty mines in the Kattegat. The aim was the destruction of German shipping.

Captain J. S. Bethell, based at Rosyth, was in charge of the flotilla of submarines that included *Seal*. After he had examined the secret orders for Operation FD7, he made a special journey to London to meet with Horton, who was known to be somewhat ferocious, in order to protest against the plans. This was an unusual thing to do. Bethell argued that, at 1,520 tons (53,200 cubic feet or 1,505 cubic metres), *Seal* was too big to enter the shallow Kattegat. Moreover, enemy aircraft and ships constantly patrolled the area. It was also known that the Germans had protected the Kattegat with mines that were attached to the seabed by cables so that they floated just below the surface of the water, waiting to explode on contact with an unsuspecting ship or submarine. It was altogether too hazardous.

Horton would not reconsider. In his opinion the overall war situation justified the risk. Bethell returned to his base privately convinced that *Seal* would never return from Operation FD7.

Ignorant of all this activity behind the scenes, *Seal* sailed from Immingham on Monday, 29 April 1940. The fifty mines were laid in the appointed area on 4 May. Eight tons (8,128 kg.) of British mines now formed a barrier across the southern end of the Kattegat—exactly as Horton had planned. That was a serious obstacle to enemy shipping, as some merchant vessels found out to their cost. One thing remained for *Seal* to do—reach home.

As Lonsdale and his men tried to make their escape, enemy aircraft spotted *Seal*. To avoid them, she dived at 02.27. The aircraft responded by calling in specially equipped German boats to attack her. These were similar to small trawlers, and called UJ boats, the name being taken from *U-Jägers*, meaning 'submarine hunters'. UJ boats had underwater hydrophone listening equipment. To listen for a submarine's engines these boats had to stop. *Seal* therefore watched them from underwater using the periscope. Whenever they stopped to listen for the noise of *Seal's* engines, Lonsdale would quickly order the engines to be switched off. It became a grim game of under-water hide and seek, with the hunters coming a little closer all the time.

Seal had been underwater for sixteen hours. She had achieved success. It appeared that she had shaken off her pursuers. The crew relaxed. Food was the order of the day. The menu was roast beef, potatoes and peas, to be followed by prunes and custard. At about 19.00, in the early evening of 4 May, came the unexpected reverberation of a violent explosion. The mooring cable of a German mine had scraped along the hull, and the floating mine, which they had no way of seeing, had torn open the rear of the hull. Everything—men, equipment and food—flew in all directions. *Seal's* stern was severely damaged and, out of control, she slowly sank ninety feet (twenty-seven metres or more) to the seabed.

The two flooded rear compartments were immediately sealed off. The crew's best estimate was that about 130 tons (4,550 cubic feet or 129 cubic metres) of water had entered the stern of the boat. There was no panic. Lonsdale, in the control room, was at the centre of the scene. He remained calm, alert and focused. The weight of the crew's trust was on him. Their lives were in his hands. What would he do? It was a crushingly lonely time for the commander.

The obvious thing was to wait until all daylight had gone and try to reach the surface from the seabed. At 22.30 Lonsdale ordered, 'Stand by to surface,' followed by the command: 'Surface.' The stricken boat started to rise. Every man in the crew was tense. But then *Seal* slowly sank back to the sea floor. The problem was that the weight of the water inside the boat was pressing the damaged stern down hard into the mud. The bow was pointing upwards to the water's surface at an angle of twenty-five degrees.

They made several more attempts to surface. *Seal* would not budge. Every man on board knew that they were in deep trouble. There was no ventilation. The air was becoming foul. The combined smells of sweat, disinfectant, oil, tea, rum and various types of uneaten food were utterly nauseating, even to the strongest stomach. Condensation dripped from every part of the metal hull. Most men had fierce headaches, thumping hearts and sickness. One man, amazed at his own heartbeat, took his pulse and found it twice its normal rate—and that was while he was sitting still. All, even in a seating position, were gasping for air. To take three paces had the same effect as a hundred-yard sprint under normal conditions.

The crew members were used to danger, but not to this. The idea of dying slowly from carbon dioxide poisoning was a horrible thought. They had all known men in other submarines who had failed to return from a patrol. Such friends had braved the depths of the sea and had lost. It was always something that happened to another crew; now it was their turn. Throughout the boat, men apathetically accepted that death was inevitable. They had failed. They were helpless. *Seal* was no more than their metal coffin.

It was 01.10 on 5 May 1940. Twenty-three hours had passed since *Seal* had dived. They had reached the end of all human resources. Lonsdale turned to those around him in the control room: 'We have tried everything we can think of to get to the surface, but without result. None of us can think of anything else. We have all run out of ideas. So I am going to call the crew together and we shall say some simple prayers. Our object will be to ask God to help us.' For years Lonsdale had implicitly believed the truth of the Bible's words: 'All things are possible with God' (Mark 10:27).

The very idea of praying stirred the weary crew of *Seal*, who

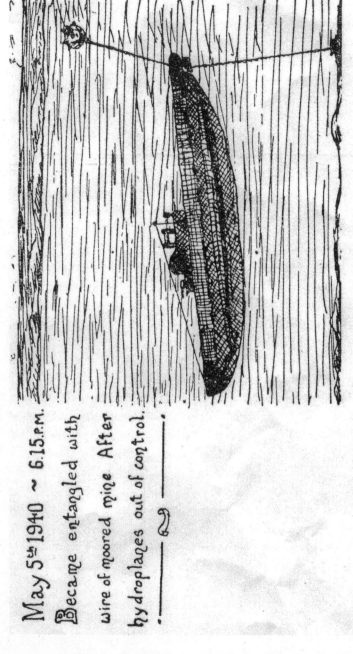

May 5th 1940 ~ 6.15.p.m.
Became entangled with
wire of moored mine. After
hydroplanes out of control.

Sketch drawn by Signalman Waddington to show Seal's predicament (probably drawn while sunk in the Kattegat). Note the error in the date: 'May 5th' should be 'May 4th'.

were scattered about the stricken submarine. Some felt easier in themselves at the thought of praying to God. Two men out of fifty-nine refused to pray. 'I don't consider you can surface a boat by praying,' grunted 'Tubby' Lister. Stoker Eckersall agreed with him. Wearing a navy-blue roll-neck sweater and jacket, Lonsdale looked 'reassuring' to those who could see him.

This is how he began: 'We have been in some tight spots before and we've come through. With God's help we shall do so again. I think it is time we said the Lord's Prayer together; but first I want to ask God to help us.'

'Dear God,' he prayed, 'we have tried everything in our power to save ourselves and we have failed. Yet we believe that you can do things that are impossible to men. Please, O Lord, deliver us.' Lonsdale started the Lord's Prayer and found himself joined with a lot of voices more full of reverence and feeling than he had ever believed possible. The sounds of praying stopped. Lonsdale continued, 'And now, I think we should all quietly say our own prayers to God.'[1] He stood silent, head bowed, to lead his men again. Finally, the impromptu service was over.

The answer to their prayers came almost immediately.

Lonsdale had an idea that had occurred to him alone. He acted like a reinvigorated man. For his new orders to be obeyed, he needed a response from his crew. Although they were feeling half dead, they rallied to his orders. He wanted a rope rigged up along the length of the sloping submarine. Every man not needed for the very last attempt to surface was told to move up the slope, holding on to the rope, and go as far as he could into the forward part of *Seal*. Lonsdale was using his men as human ballast. It seemed a poor hope to depend on the combined weight of about fifty men at the front of the submarine to provide enough leverage to loosen the stern, which was so firmly stuck in the mud. Though every step up the slope seemed like a mile, it was done. Heads felt as if they had pneumatic drills vibrating in them. The forward compartments filled with men, too weak to talk or sit up. Most of them had secretly come to terms with death earlier. A few managed weak and unconvincing smiles at one another.

Soon after 01.30 Lonsdale gave the final orders. The last two tanks were blown. The engines ran at maximum power. Slowly, agonizingly, *Seal* shuddered from end to end. Then she broke free from the seabed. The boat levelled out and, ever so slowly, moved upwards. The vibrations stopped. Men could hear the lapping of surface water against the hull. 'She's up! She's up!' shouted one young crewman in excitement. Lonsdale's voice interrupted: 'We have surfaced. Everyone will stay exactly where he is until I call my instructions from the bridge.'

The captain's lifestyle of prayer had long included brief 'arrow' prayers that nobody knew about. Now he whispered, 'Thank you, Lord.' Most of the crew, both then and later, believed that they had experienced a definite miracle of kindly divine providence. Even the non-praying Stoker Eckersall was spiritually changed.

If Lonsdale had opened the hatch straight away the pressure that had built up over twenty-three hours would have catapulted him up into the air, clean out of the boat. Taking the necessary precautions, he slowly opened the hatch. A wave of fresh air blew into *Seal*. A group of men embraced one another like jubilant members of a football team after a goal has been scored.

At 02.10 Lonsdale sent a coded message from *Seal* to England explaining the situation. It said:

Most immediate. Confidential.

Seal to Vice-Admiral Submarines.

Submarine filled with water from stern to 129 bulkhead, caused by mine or depth charge. FD7 in position. Secret

May 6th 1940. ~ 1.10 A.M.
Final attempt to surface.
Last two tanks were blown.
Motors to full speed ahead.
At last she began to move,
she was leaving the
bottom. All compressed air
practically expended.

Sketch drawn by Signalman Waddington depicting the final attempt to raise Seal.
Note the error in the date: 'May 6th' should be 'May 5th'

books destroyed. Am making for Swedish coast. Will try for
Gothenburg.

Once *Seal* was on the surface, the onslaught from German
aircraft was devastating. At one stage a cannon shell cut the
boat's voice-pipe in half as Lonsdale was shouting orders into it.
He carried on, seemingly unperturbed. Before long *Seal* was dead
in the water. The idea of reaching neutral Sweden was plainly
impossible. Lieutenant Karl Schmidt, an officer aboard a circling
German Arado 196 floatplane, looked down and thought she
looked like a mortally wounded whale. He felt thankful that he
was an airman, not a submariner.

All secret equipment was now destroyed in accordance with
standard naval procedures. As a result, Lonsdale never received
the return message from the Admiralty. This informed him that
in the circumstances the safety of his men should be his primary
consideration. Those orders gave him the official authority for
what he had already decided to do.

The floatplane landed alongside. Before taking the dive to swim
to the enemy aircraft, Lonsdale made the decision to let his men
live. *Seal* had been fitted with two explosive charges in her bilges
that would automatically explode if they scuttled the boat and the
men took to the water. Several of his men were badly wounded
and would not survive if they were to try to swim in such cold
water. Lonsdale calculated that if the charges were detonated as
Seal sank, every man would be blown to pieces in the water. Quite
reasonably, Lonsdale thought *Seal* would probably sink of her own
accord if the Germans made any attempt to tow her to port as a
prize.

Lieutenant Beet, now in command of *Seal*, knew of Lonsdale's
wish to save the crew. Surrender was the only way to save them.
UJ 128, one of the submarine-killing trawlers, arrived and took off
Seal's crew at 06.30. At that moment *Seal* became the first British

Dear God, we have tried everything in our power to save ourselves and we have failed. Yet we believe that You can do all things which are impossible to men. Please, O Lord, deliver us.

Lieutenant-Commander Rupert Lonsdale. May 1940

They saw the works of the LORD, his wonderful deeds in the deep.

Psalm 107:24

The story of the deliverance of Seal moved artist Peter Millward to create this impression.

vessel to surrender to the enemy since a warship was forced to surrender to the American ship *Wasp* in the war of 1812.

The Germans towed the punctured *Seal* back to port. Lonsdale knew none of this until, to his horror, he caught a glimpse of her at Kiel, where he was held prisoner for a time. German propaganda made a great deal of the capture, as well they might. However, the plan to re-equip *Seal*, commission her into the German Navy and use her to attack the British proved impossible. Eventually the Germans themselves scuttled her, and an RAF bomb did the rest.

During five years in various prison camps, the prisoners were supported in every way possible by the people of the village of Seal, near Sevenoaks in Kent. After release, the crew visited the village to express their thanks. Lonsdale found himself facing, not only friendly faces, but also the standard court martial for an officer who had lost his boat to the enemy. After only thirty minutes he was acquitted with honour. His decision to save the lives of his men, even at the risk of the boat's capture, was vindicated. To his surprise he was treated as a hero and later promoted to the rank of commander.

By the time of the trial, his heart was elsewhere. Prison had given him time to think seriously about life. Services in camp gave him his first opportunity to preach. His faith in Christ deepened. His knowledge of the Bible increased. The call of the Christian ministry was overwhelming. He trained to be a Church of England minister at Ridley Hall, Cambridge, and was ordained in 1949. He preached the biblical gospel in English churches in Dorset, Hampshire and Norfolk. For many years he ministered in Kenya. Long after his official retirement in 1970, he preached in Madrid, Lisbon and Tenerife.

Asked to define his basic beliefs, he replied to the writer with these words:

I don't see how anyone cannot believe that there is a

Power who created the universe. Some Mind must have created the orderliness of the stars and the solar system. Consider the phases of the moon; the regularity of the tides and seasons; the implanting of a magnetic North Pole; the fact of gravity; all point to the infinite Master Mind beyond our understanding in greatness.

The Bible tells us that evil has entered into this creation. I believe in the everlasting mercy and patience of God, though if people carry on being rebels against God, it must end in being put out of his kingdom.

I believe in Christ as the Son of God. No man ever spoke or acted as he did. His power over evil, his wisdom and love show that he was above all other men. He was the true image of God. Yet he was a man knowing weariness, frustration and suffering—tempted like us, yet without sin. Those around him knew these truths.

The Bible tells us all this and I believe the Bible is true. Christ showed us what God is like. By faith in Christ Christians have forgiveness and eternal life. Heaven is unspoilt by evil. Those who have never received God's forgiveness may not take their unforgiven sin into God's holy presence after death. During this life real believers grow more into Christ's likeness.

I also believe in the Devil, cunning, strong, always ready to draw us away from being fashioned by God. The Devil can be successfully resisted when we ask for God's help.

Nothing will ever shake me from my belief that God is love, despite the things I have seen happen to other people in the war, not to mention the things that have happened to me.

I believe God has a plan for each one of us and we must put our lives in his hands.

More needs to be written about the Holy Spirit, the cross and the fact of the resurrection which are the heart of my faith ...

The crew of *Seal* stuck together in the years after the war. When people are bonded together by some hard experience this sometimes happens. Lonsdale's men never forgot him. And he never failed to keep in touch with them. It was more than just an annual Christmas card for all of them. Lonsdale knew that they had prayed to be rescued from death at the bottom of the sea. He also knew for certain that many of his men found real faith in Christ as a result of that desperate experience of seeking the Lord.

In 1960, Rupert Lonsdale was asked to cooperate in the production of a book about what had happened to *Seal*. The authors, Jim Warren and James Benson, had already written *Above us the Waves*. That book was made into a fine film. Lonsdale supplied information only on condition that the place of Christ in his life was openly acknowledged. The words of the book's title, *Will Not We Fear*, come from Psalm 46:2 in the Authorized or King James Version of the Bible. This passage is printed in full before the title page of the book. Then comes a foreword by 'Rev. R. P Lonsdale'. He records that he only agreed to become involved in the project in the hope that some readers might come to faith in God through reading the book. After its publication he received letters from readers saying precisely that.

In 1986, when Lonsdale was eighty-one, this writer received a letter from him in which he said that he wanted to print the testimonies of seventy of his Christian friends. It was an evangelistic enterprise. Not one of his friends failed to contribute. The resulting booklet has a preface written by Lonsdale that warns against having a second-hand faith. It says, 'We are all sinners and the Bible tells us that Jesus receives sinners. None can be too bad. Jesus said, "The person who comes to me I will in no wise cast out." It is only because of who Christ is, and what he has done, that we can be saved. If we have as many good deeds to boast of as there are grains of sand upon the shore, but do not have Christ, we have no hope. We should not wait until we are better before we come to Christ. Come now.'[2]

To Lonsdale's astonishment, 5,000 booklets were distributed quickly. At least a thousand were read in prisons. Then followed another 5,000 copies. He would not charge for them and nobody ever found out where the money for the printing and production came from.

After the war was over, Lonsdale remarried. Kathleen, his second wife, died of cancer in 1961. His third wife, Ursula, died of a brain tumour in 1986. Over his study desk he hung a painting with the words, 'Faith sees through tears,' written below it. The trials of his personal life served to deepen his trust in the Lord. 'When I am down,' he wrote, 'I find that kneeling and giving my life and problems to God enables me to find him and his grace.'

Rupert Philip Lonsdale witnessed for Christ in submarines, in prisoner-of-war camps, in Ridley Hall and in more than half a dozen churches where he was minister. Those who knew him often commented on his humility. He wanted to be forgotten because he felt that he was just one more very ordinary person. Yet those who know the story of the submarine *Seal*, and the part his faith in God played in saving its crew, find him unforgettable.

Lonsdale fought the good fight, kept the faith and finished the course. He died in Bournemouth in 1999 aged ninety-three.

More information on Rupert Lonsdale

My correspondence with Rupert Lonsdale pre-dated a visit made to him at his Wiltshire home in August 1975. He was a constant spiritual inspiration.

The book *Will Not We Fear* (1961), good though it is, should be read with other sources. Captain S. W. Roskill, the Royal Navy's official historian, wrote *The Secret Capture* (1959). A letter from Lonsdale is printed in the text of this book. Lonsdale's obituary in the *Daily Telegraph* (15 May 1999) contains information not available elsewhere and is excellent apart from the fact that the writer underplays his spirituality. The same comment is true of the report in the *Independent* (13 May 1999). Items on the Internet giving factual details relating to *Seal* are usually accurate, but not so reliable on spiritual matters.

His widow Ethné and son Dr John Lonsdale, a retired history lecturer from Cambridge, survive Rupert Lonsdale. Both have helped me with pictures and information, for which I express my thanks.

10

Donald Caskie

The Tartan Pimpernel

He opened the door to his rooms, flicked on the light, turned round and found himself with five revolvers pointing at him. The faces behind the guns were serious and unsmiling. One voice said, 'Pastor Caskie, you are under arrest. You must come with us—now.'

Donald Caskie in chaplain's uniform, 1944/1945

10

Donald Caskie

I t was Sunday, 9 June 1940. The congregation in the Scots Presbyterian Church in Rue Bayard, Paris, could hear the sound of the distant guns of the approaching and all-conquering German Army.

Donald Caskie, the thirty-eight-year-old minister, knew that he would be a marked man when Hitler's troops entered Paris. Frequently in his sermons he had denounced both Nazi ideology and Germany's obviously warlike intentions. One of his particular targets was their racial persecution. When news of the atrocities in the concentration camps reached him, he had condemned what was being done to the innocent. French spies in the pay of the Nazis sometimes sat amongst his congregation and had heard him say that Hitler had 'sown the wind and would reap the whirlwind'.

When that morning service was over, he took a last look round the church building. There on a table near the exit was a bunch of white heather. He had brought it from his native island the previous year. As he locked the church he wondered whether he would ever see his real home again.

His friend Gaston, who owned the café next door, agreed to

look after the keys to the church. Gaston had decided to remain in
Paris, and would witness the pomp and arrogance of the victorious
German Army as it marched into the city in triumph a few days
later.

With a bag on his back and sadness in his heart, Donald Caskie
joined the great exodus of miserable crowds escaping from Paris.
First walking, then cycling, he headed for the south of France.
Several times, diving German planes bombed and shot at people
on the roads. Men, women and children were needlessly killed
before his eyes as a consequence of this random strafing.

After a very eventful journey, Caskie arrived at Bayonne, a port
on the south-west coast. To his relief, the British consulate was
open. The last ship for Britain would be leaving in a few hours'
time and there was a place on board for him. In his mind he could
already see the peaceful safety of Britain, but his heart was uneasy.
Surely men wounded in the fighting had a moral right to priority?
God had called him to minister in France. Was he prepared to let
the Nazis frighten him away?

He heard himself tell the consular officials that he would not be
going. Urgently, they asked him to reconsider his decision. There
was an inner call in his heart which they would never understand.
With mixed feelings he watched the last ship steam out of
Bayonne. Then news came through that France had surrendered.
Sadly, the new French government was willing to cooperate with
the victorious Germans. As part of the armistice arrangements,
it was agreed that German troops would occupy the entire north
and the west coast of France. There would be an unoccupied area
of France that history has called 'Vichy' France. German troops
would not enter this area providing the French authorities carried
out Nazi policies. In this way the French government cooperated
with the Nazis until November 1942, when Hitler brought the
arrangement to an end by taking over all of France.

One condition imposed by the Nazis was the insistence that

the French must capture and imprison any British troops who had escaped to the south during the confused fighting in the north. The greatest part of the British Army had been rescued by the Royal Navy from the beaches of Dunkirk—and taken across the English Channel to safety.

Caskie was informed that many of the men who had not escaped had found their way to the south coast of France, particularly to the port of Marseilles. Hearing that, he found transport to take him south-east to Marseilles. To his horror there were many thousands of British soldiers on the seafront. Quite a few were wounded. All were battle-stained, exhausted and lacking direction. The local French government and people would give them no food or help. Worse, soon they would be arrested by the French, merely to please the Germans.

To Caskie the troops looked like 'sheep without a shepherd'. The conviction grew that God wanted to use him to minister to the needs of these men and, if possible, help them to escape.

It was the summer of 1940. America was still a neutral country and the American Consul was looking after British interests in France. To Caskie's delight, the US consulate offered to supply as many identity cards as he required. They were British identity documents with an imposing American seal, heavily embossed and ornate. All he had to do was distribute them to the British soldiers to fill in and the men would have secure civilian identity papers. The consulate also suggested that he take over a deserted building nearby—the British and American Seamen's Mission at 46 Rue de Forbin.

Aflame with a strong sense of urgency, Caskie nailed up a big notice on the wall of the mission. It said, 'Now open to British civilians and seamen only.' He threw open the doors with a flourish, angry that men who had come to fight for France would now be imprisoned like animals unless something was done to help. Before long the mission was crowded with British

soldiers whose uniforms had to be destroyed as soon as possible
to save them from arrest by the new pro-Nazi French police. The
desperate British troops had to change into second-hand civilian
clothing, initially supplied by local Greek and Cypriot merchants
from downtown Marseilles. Their original British uniforms were
dumped in the sea.

Having saved them from prison by passing them off as civilians,
Caskie's biggest problem was how to get them over the border
into neutral Spain, and so to freedom via Gibraltar. Throughout
the summer of 1940 more and more British troops arrived. They
packed the chapel of the former Seamen's Mission as he conducted
much-appreciated services of Christian worship.

His unexpected activities reached the ears of a branch of British
Military Intelligence, MI9. Caskie was no secret agent. He had
no experience of escape lines. He relied on the Bible and prayer
to God to shape the way he acted. 'My only armour was the grace
of God and my native gumption,' was how he put it later. It was
nerve-wracking, because the French police raided the mission
regularly to make sure there were no British servicemen present.
With the help of MI9, guides were found. Sometimes British secret
agents would visit him with advice and money.

For his part, Caskie kept records in Gaelic, which the enemy
would not be able to read even if they found the papers. He took
down each man's name, address, service number, regiment and
the name and address of his next of kin. As a result he could
send telegrams via Lisbon in neutral Portugal to the Church
of Scotland offices in Edinburgh. These telegrams would say
something like this: 'Tell Thomson, No. X. Tollcross, Edinburgh,
that Jock ... number ..., Seaforth Highlanders, is safe with me.'[1] In
this way hundreds of families all over Britain received unexpected
reassurance from the Church of Scotland offices that their men
were alive and well.

One cockney soldier, Corporal Alf Smith, found seven ration

cards in a gutter. That would have provided a way of feeding seven men. Caskie examined the cards and observed that they belonged to a French widow, Madame Jeanne Tillois, who had six children to feed. Caskie insisted that his work would not have God's blessing if he took advantage of another person's loss.

When he returned the cards to the owner, he discovered that Madame Tillois was an evangelical Christian. She was a member of the local Reformed Evangelical Church led by Pastor Heuzy. This good man had worked as a pastor in Glasgow for many years before the war. As a result he had an unusual Franco-Scottish accent when he spoke English. His assessment of the new forces that controlled Germany was shrewd. He took the view that the Nazis produced 'professional evil-doers'.

Never in Caskie's life did an honest action bring so great a reward. Pastor Heuzy and his people were all anti-Nazi. Like all Christian congregations, they were a varied group: professional men, factory workers, intellectuals, old and young. They were prayerful, godly folk from the historic French Reformed tradition. Pastor Heuzy and his congregation became a vital link in the emerging escape route. They provided parcels of civilian clothes, compasses, maps and other escape materials. Some even hid British escapers in their homes for short periods.

By the winter of 1940–41, British agents had integrated the Seamen's Mission into the PAT escape line, named after the agent known as Pat O'Leary (this was not his real name). By that winter the line was operating like a well-oiled machine. Men were regularly smuggled into Spain and so to freedom. One MI9 agent, Airey Neave, who himself escaped from Colditz prisoner-of-war camp, later estimated that the PAT line aided at least 600 men to liberty.

For Donald Caskie, the whole experience of helping men to freedom was ultimately a matter of dependence on God and the outworking of his Christian faith. Often he describes sinking to his knees and turning circumstances over to his Heavenly Father. 'Dear God,' he would pray, 'you think this out for me please. I'm beaten.' As he relied on the Lord and his regular reading of the Bible, he experienced answers to prayer, guidance in dealing with difficult situations and, on occasion, unusual insights which he believed were given him by God.

There was also Christian pastoral work to do. For instance, one escaping soldier, David, walked 600 miles to reach the safety of the Seamen's Mission. At night he would wake other men by screaming in his sleep. Eventually this troubled man told Caskie about his inner turmoil. He was the only son of a widow and a member of a small Christian church in Yorkshire. While in prison he was amazed to discover that one of the German guards was a Christian from the same denomination as his own. They became friends. The German guard allotted David a job, but while he was supposed to be carrying out this task he seized the opportunity to make his escape.

David had not gone far when a German soldier on a bicycle grew suspicious and, dismounting, walked towards David's hiding place. The soldier's hand was on his pistol, ready to use it. David realized he was hiding on a building site and, as the German approached, he grabbed a long iron bar and began beating the soldier on the head until he dropped down dead. To his horror, David then found himself staring into the face of the kind German who had helped him. Images of the dead man's face continued to haunt him afterwards and deeply disturbed his mind.'

David's trauma did not last long, however, because as he was one of a party heading for freedom across the Spanish frontier, the group was deliberately led into a trap and he was among those who were shot as a consequence.

For some time Caskie had had an unsettling belief that one of the guides on the route into Spain was a traitor. He had told Pat O'Leary his view that Harold Cole was a double agent working for the enemy as well as the British, but he had to abide by the decisions of those who ran the escape line. Yet the doubts about Cole continued to nag him and were eventually shown to be true. After the war was over, a book was written about Cole, which was given the subtitle *The Worst Traitor of the War*.

Cole's treachery led to many tragedies. Pastor Heuzy had been under suspicion for some time. The Gestapo, the German state secret police, shot this godly man. At least 500 British servicemen had their 'cover' blown wide open. Some were shot as 'spies' because they were wearing civilian clothes. The others were imprisoned.

For Caskie, this marked the end of his work at the Seamen's Mission. Already in April 1941 he had been arrested by the unnecessarily cruel Vichy French police, questioned, warned, but then released. This time he was put on trial before a French 'military tribunal' meeting in a room at the old Fort St Nicholas. He was sentenced to two years' imprisonment. Fortunately for him, it was only to be served if he offended again. The judge ordered the Seamen's Mission to close within ten days. Caskie himself was instructed to remove himself from Marseilles. The judge suggested that he should go to Grenoble.

A few days after his trial, a British agent arrived at the Seamen's Mission. 'Padre', he said, 'we know all about your trial and condemnation and we feel sure that from now on your life will be in danger. A plane will take off from an airfield near Arles in a day or two, and I have been told to offer you a flight to England.' However, by this time Caskie was even more firmly convinced that the Lord wanted him in France. The pilot arrived safely in England—without Donald Caskie.

He was destined to spend two years in Grenoble. Noting his impressive academic qualifications, the University of Grenoble appointed him as visiting Professor of English. That provided him with an income. He also preached regularly in local French

Reformed churches. His time became balanced between preaching and study, on the one hand, and helping MI9, on the other. Once a month he visited the prison at St Hippolyte near Nimes to preach and take a communion service. This was a seventeen-hour journey by train. As chaplain to British prisoners of war, he would bring the solace and challenge of gospel preaching. At the same time he smuggled in files, scissors, small crowbars and false identity papers.

To a few men audacity is almost an instinct. They take to risk and adventure as easily as a swallow takes to the air. One man Caskie put in this category was the American-born Battle of Britain pilot Whitney Straight. Caskie's work in helping the imprisoned pilot to reach England was successful. On this occasion they used 'the medical swindle'. This involved the prisoner's swallowing enough pills—often aspirin—to make him appear genuinely ill. Whitney Straight was taken from La Turbie Prison near Monte Carlo to the local hospital. From there it was much easier to escape.

However, such constant danger put an unaccustomed strain on Caskie. He was becoming seriously overtired and stressed. Yet again a British MI9 agent warned him that he was in imminent danger of arrest. His advice was to board an RAF plane on a secret mission, which would land in a field near Grenoble. It was scheduled to land on the very day the warning was given. The agent added, 'You will be in England before breakfast.'

Caskie's decision came easily to him—he would remain in France. As far as he was concerned, he was obeying the call of God. Later he wrote, 'Before I slept each night, I beseeched God to help us and thanked him for the guidance that stopped me accepting the offer of a return to England.'

It was now April 1943, a month of glorious sunshine. Caskie did not know that he had helped his last prisoner of war to escape. He always recalled that man's name, William Nash from Whitburn. Hardly was Nash free before Caskie was in captivity.

16 April was especially memorable. It was a warm spring night. Caskie returned to his lodgings in Grenoble, praying all the time as he walked down the road. He opened the door to his rooms, flicked on the light, turned round and found himself with five revolvers pointing at him. The faces behind the guns were serious and unsmiling. One voice said, 'Pastor Caskie, you are under arrest. You must come with us—now.' He was handcuffed. At first it seemed faintly amusing that it took five armed men to arrest the 'little minister', as some Scottish escapers called him. What was to come, however, was far from humorous.

Donald Caskie was imprisoned without trial, first by the Italians, then by the Germans. When his Bible was taken from him, he relied on his childhood training. At that time he had memorized whole chapters and complete psalms. 'My knowledge of the Scriptures saved me,' was his later assessment. Long hours were spent in solitary confinement, living on dry bread and water. Besides recalling long Bible passages, he began to comfort himself by thinking back to his early life, which had begun in a very different place.

Born in 1902, at Bowmore on the island of Islay, off the west coast of Scotland, he had six brothers and one sister. His father was a poor crofter. Spiritually, however, the members of the family were millionaires. Family worship in a godly Presbyterian home of the time was taken for granted, but it was also made clear that real Christian faith, being born again, is a most personal matter.

In a letter to this writer Donald Caskie wrote the following about his conversion: 'One evening, after a time of searching, I knelt down at my bedside and surrendered myself to Christ. The words which came to me as I knelt that night were words which our minister uttered at the close of his sermon: "Whoever comes to me I will never turn away." There was nothing emotional or spectacular about it. This simple act of faith completely changed my life, and made me, and all things, new.'

His mother had prayed that at least one of her children would become a minister, and noticed with interest how even as a child Donald would stand on a stool and 'preach' to his reluctant brothers.

After school at Dunoon, he studied at Edinburgh University, receiving his MA in 1926. Training for the ministry took place in the same city at New College. After preaching at Dauphin Plains in Manitoba, Canada, he engaged in archaeological research work in Libya for the University of Michigan. Finally he was ordained in 1932 and his first three-year period of ministry was at Gretna Green, just north of Carlisle. Here Caskie, the lifelong bachelor, found himself marrying runaway couples who preferred Scots to English law. At the time, Scots law favoured the runaways.

In 1935 he transferred to the Scots Church in Paris. It was this move to Paris that would eventually pitch him into difficulties with the Nazis which nobody could have foreseen.

One of the consequences involved being held in seven prisons in 1943–44. One was the Villa Lynwood in Nice. On that beautiful coast in times of peace it had been the property of a well-to-do English lady. When Caskie was there in May 1943, it had been turned into a house of torture surrounded by barbed wire. Heavily armed men guarded every entrance. Dogs wandered loose in the garden at night. From his cell he heard screams that were distressing to a gentle pastor.

The diet was stale bread and water. There were signatures etched on the plaster of the cell wall. Some had been written by men he knew to be dead. With his long, uncut nails he carved his name and added some verses from Isaiah in English:

> Thus saith the LORD ... Fear not: for I have redeemed thee,
> I have called thee by thy name; thou art mine. When thou

passest through the waters, I will be with thee; and through the rivers, they shall not overflow thee: when thou walkest through the fire, thou shalt not be burned; neither shall the flame kindle upon thee' (Isaiah 43:1–3, AV).

He had run out of fingernails and plaster space. Then he solemnly prayed that the Holy Spirit would use the words to meet the need of some tired soul in need of the peace of God.

A Frenchman, Captain Vallet, followed Caskie in the same cell. Afraid of torture, Vallet was about to open one of his veins and kill himself, when he caught sight of the words inscribed on the plaster. The Word of God spoke to him, settled his mind and saved his life. Not long after this incident, Vallet and Caskie shared a prison cell at San Remo in Italy. The soldier told Caskie about the words that had prevented his suicide. 'I will never forget those words,' he said. To prove it, he recited them from memory. Caskie's prayer had been answered.

In mid-August he was taken in chains by train to the prison of Fresnes on the southern outskirts of Paris. The next major test was to face a tough Gestapo 'trial' in a building on the Rue des Saussaies, strangely enough only a short distance from the closed British Embassy in Paris. They took him from his cell on 26 November 1943. For eight exhausting hours he was accused of being a spy, an agitator, an agent for escaping soldiers and other prisoners of war. The final crime was being friendly towards the Jews. Pierre, one of the guides used during his days at the Seamen's Mission in Marseilles, gave evidence against him. Asked if he recognized Pierre, Caskie asserted that he recognized him as a double agent in the category of Judas Iscariot. He had known for a long time that by no means all the French population opposed the German occupying power. The result was inevitable. He was sentenced to death.

Before his execution he asked the prison authorities if he might consult a Christian minister. Next day, Pastor Hans Helmut Peters came into the cell. To Caskie's astonishment, he was a Bible-believing Lutheran. The two men found that they were real brothers in Christ. Peters read the closing verses of Romans chapter 8, prayed and conducted a communion service in the cell.

Peters promised that he would do all in his power to have the death sentence commuted to life imprisonment. For the next seven weeks in Fresnes, Caskie daily expected death. During this time, many fellow prisoners were dragged away and executed.

On 7 January 1944 news reached him that the death sentence had been lifted. Although we cannot be certain, it is likely that those whom Peters had spoken to on his behalf included, among others, the anti-Nazi Major-General Dr Hans Speidel, Field Marshal Rommel's second in command, and possibly also some German officers who later lost their own lives after the unsuccessful attempt on Hitler's life in July 1944.

Caskie was moved to St Denis prison in Paris, where a more relaxed regime awaited him. In secret, the prisoners listened to the BBC. They knew about the Allied invasion of Normandy on D-Day, 6 June 1944. Many prayed for its success. Almost everybody was convinced that for Hitler 'the writing was on the wall'. Finally, in August 1944, the triumphant Allies set Paris, and Donald Caskie, free. Now the exodus from Paris was going in the opposite direction—towards Germany.

Though liberated, Caskie still refused to return to Britain. There was a ministry for him in France. His first act was to see if Gaston, the café owner, still had the keys to the church from which he had fled in June 1940. After an emotional reunion, the precious keys were returned. The church building remained as he had left it in 1940, dusty but otherwise untouched. The bunch of white heather he had left on a table remained in the same place. Donald Caskie sank to his knees in the silence and thanked God for bringing him through many troubles and dangers to the safety of this special moment.

The British Intelligence Service now asked to see him. He was asked to identify one particular prisoner. To his amazement, it was Harold Cole, the traitor who had exploited the war for his own gain. Shortly afterwards, Cole would die trying to shoot his way out of trouble.

As for Caskie, he became an army chaplain in addition to ministering the Word of God in his church. On the day of liberation from the Nazis, he wrote, 'My happiness can only be imagined; it cannot be described.'

On the first Sunday of freedom, he led worship, preached and finally walked out of the Scots Church in Rue Bayard to be greeted from the turret of a passing tank by a soldier he had rescued from Marseilles three years earlier. After that joyful service, the surprise at seeing his old friend nearly reduced Caskie to tears. Casting restraint aside, he jumped up onto the tank as it rumbled on towards the Champs-Elysées. In the August sun, the surging crowds of French people gave a highly emotional welcome to the deliverers. The Nazis had gone and were not coming back.

A new stage of his life was beginning. Donald Caskie had not been home since 1937. As 1944 drew to a close he was flown back to southern England. At Dunsfold airfield in Surrey, he felt so overwhelmed by emotion that he kissed the ground and thanked the Lord that he was home again—and in one piece. On the BBC news that night it was broadcast that Donald Caskie, 'The Tartan Pimpernel', had arrived in Britain.

For his wartime work, King George VI awarded him the OBE. His old university awarded him the degree of Doctor of Divinity. In 1959 he appeared on the TV programme *This Is Your Life* where he was reunited with Peters and with many people who had shared his early life and his wartime activities. A big red book recording the main features of his life was presented to him after the programme was over. Those who are interested can still see it in the National Library of Scotland in Edinburgh. Unfortunately, a 1950s project for a film, with actor Richard Todd playing Caskie, had to be shelved because of financial difficulties in the British film industry.

His Christian ministry continued in Paris until 1960. There were subsequent ministries in two Scottish parishes until he retired in 1968. During retirement, he became well known in Christian circles in Edinburgh. Derek Prime, a local minister at the time, wrote a pen portrait of him for me in which he says, 'Donald Caskie was a delightful man, well-known and loved in the city. Sometimes he would come to Sunday evening services at the Chapel where I served. He loved the gospel emphasis and showed his appreciation of it … I would underline his personal warmth.

Donald Caskie receives his 'big red book' from host Eamonn Andrews at the end of This is Your Life *in 1959.*

I remember his catching sight of me on a train travelling to the north of Scotland, and his wanting to sit and talk with me.'

Caskie's book, *The Tartan Pimpernel*, was first published in 1957. Since it is a true account, it is far more exciting than the merely fictional *Scarlet Pimpernel*, and since it is written by a Christian, it emphasizes the sovereignty of the loving, caring God in whom he trusted.

In later correspondence, the writer asked Donald Caskie to state his most basic conviction in a sentence. The answer he gave is this: 'My most basic Christian belief is that God is our Father, that he sent his Son, Jesus Christ, into the world for us and our salvation, and that if we believe in him and receive him by faith into our hearts, he will save us and keep us, use us in his service, and make us a blessing to others.'

In that faith he died in 1983 aged eighty-one. His grave is located in the isolated Church of Scotland cemetery at Bowmore on the Isle of Islay. Apart from mentioning that he was known as 'The Tartan Pimpernel', the headstone gives no indication of the personal faith that motivated him, or any clue to the adventurous life he lived in the service of others.

More information on Donald Caskie

When I arranged to meet Dr Donald Caskie at 11.00 a.m. on 17 August 1972 at the Royal Overseas Club, Princes Street, Edinburgh, he was breathless and slightly late. He had 'bumped into' a postman who had once been a soldier on the escape line that started at Marseilles in 1940.

Caskie and I never stopped corresponding until he passed away. His letters amplify the story he told in *The Tartan Pimpernel* (Oldbourne Press, 1957). I have also had contact with surviving members of his family, one of whom unearthed photographs taken on the occasion of the *This is Your Life* TV programme. Sadly, because the programme was live no recording was made. Dr Wayne Pearce went to the National Library of Scotland and scoured the 'big red book' from *This Is Your Life* for information, as well as all Caskie's surviving papers.

During my research I was given copies of two radio programmes on which Caskie was the guest. It was my privilege to donate copies of them to the National Library of Scotland. All these sources provided information not in his book.

I would also like to express my thanks to Pastor Derek Prime for responding to my request to write about Caskie.

11

Michiharu Shinya

From prison to the pulpit

He climbed down the narrow ladder. The signal-room door was half open. He glanced in. Several signalmen sat in position, motionless—dead. At the bottom of the ladder, he could see into the wardroom. Candlelight revealed total chaos. Some men were dead; others were dying.

Michiharu Shinya when principal of Japan Biblical Seminary, 1978

11

Michiharu Shinya

The night of 12–13 November 1942 was one that Lieutenant Michiharu Shinya would never forget.

For five months the twenty-two-year-old had been torpedo officer of *Akatsuki*, a destroyer of the Imperial Japanese Navy. The naval battle of Guadalcanal was about to take place, involving fourteen Japanese ships against thirteen American vessels. Midnight had passed. The two battle fleets sailed towards each other in the darkness. Men on both sides were living on their taut nerves.

At 01.24 an American cruiser fitted with radar spotted the Japanese fleet. The ships continued to sail towards each other, neither side wanting to be seen first. *Akatsuki* was at the front, protecting the Japanese battleships.

At 01.50 *Akatsuki's* searchlight broke the darkness to light up an American cruiser. In so doing she gave away her position. At almost the same moment shells smashed into *Akatsuki*. In about fifteen minutes she sank. Only eighteen of her crew of over two hundred survived.

The ferocious sea battle that followed led to the loss of a total of

Sub-lieutenant Michiharu Shinya in 1942

eight ships, many hundreds of sailors from the opposing sides and two American admirals.

Men on both sides knew the vital necessity of the battle. After Pearl Harbor, Japanese forces had conquered an 'empire' of thousands of square miles in the Pacific leading almost to Australia. If they could control the otherwise insignificant island of Guadalcanal, they could cut the supply line from the United States to Australia. If the Allies were ever to defeat the Japanese, Australia had to be protected at all costs. Big issues were at stake.

By 02.00 Michiharu Shinya was no longer thinking about the conquest of Guadalcanal. With the explosion of the shells came a searing noise and a blinding flash. Everything shook. The blast flung him bodily onto the floor of the bridge. With a struggle he managed to sit up. Blood trickled into his right eye from a gash on his forehead. He was shell-shocked.

It had taken only one instant to shatter the boundary between reason and a state of delirium. In the darkness he had no idea of the extent of his wounds. Though still alive, he sensed impending death.

Suddenly the commanding officer shouted out, 'Port the helm.' The order was given without noticing that the helmsman was dead. So Shinya tried to obey the order. But the steering mechanism was destroyed. 'She's not responding,' he shouted. At

Akatsuki

this point he struggled to his feet. To his horror, his shoes had disappeared and the blood on the deck soaked into his socks. The slimy sensation disgusted him.

As with all ships, *Akatsuki* was controlled from the bridge. One shell had wrecked the entire control system. Only a few officers remained alive. The gunnery officer and his men were dead. All the men of the torpedo-firing section had also been wiped out—except Shinya.

Akatsuki could not hold her course. Acting on instinct, Shinya set off to try to work the auxiliary steering gear at the stern. To do this he had to squeeze through a hatch. This was blocked by a sailor's body, which he had to move. He climbed down the narrow ladder. The signal-room door was half open. He glanced in. Several signalmen sat in position, motionless—dead. At the bottom of the ladder, he could see into the wardroom. Candlelight revealed total chaos. Some men were dead; others were dying.

He looked towards the stern. Bright red flames flared out from a boiler room. The searing heat prevented him from going any further. A passing medical orderly noticed that Shinya was being blinded by blood trickling into his eye. A makeshift dressing was hurriedly fitted. He returned to the bridge feeling like a sleepwalker. The captain, the navigating officer and Shinya stood in position on the bridge. They were silent. There was no way to give orders. There were no men to obey them. The situation was hopeless.

The ships involved in the battle moved away to the west. *Akatsuki* was dead in the water. As she drifted out of control, she listed to port. The three men left on the bridge watched helplessly. Flames swept closer and closer towards them. Unable to stand erect, they propped themselves up against the ship's compass. *Akatsuki* was sinking. The surface of the sea was almost level with their eyes. The moment had come—the three men jumped from the bridge into the sea.

As Shinya struggled in the water, he watched the final moments of *Akatsuki*. The workmen of Sasebo dockyard who had built her in 1932 could never have guessed her end would be like this— sunk by Americans a few miles off the coast of Guadalcanal Island, about three thousand miles away from Japan. Shinya knew what would happen next. The sinking ship would cause survivors to be sucked down into the depths. Struggling was pointless. The violent force of the suction dragged him under. His lungs ached. He choked in the water. After what seemed a long time, he surfaced. Looking round, he could see the heads of other survivors. He grabbed one of the floating spars that the ship carried for such an emergency.

The sea battle raged on. The blue-white star shells fired by the American ships made a frightening firework display. Shells whistled past, trailing an unearthly moaning sound behind them. Suddenly the big guns fell silent. Perhaps the battle was over? The darkness and total silence were eerie. The only thought that crossed his mind was to try to swim to that part of Guadalcanal Island still held by the Japanese Army.

The pitch darkness of the night battle gave way to the morning light of 13 November. What had happened a few hours earlier seemed like a dream. Yet a glance around him showed that it was not fiction, but harsh reality. There were about thirty or forty sailors from *Akatsuki* in the water around him. Shinya made a particular search for the captain, Commander Osamu Takasuka. It was fruitless; he was never seen again.

Shinya assessed the situation. The sea was lukewarm and the sun's rays were beating down mercilessly on his head. Only now did he realize that from the head down he was covered in oil. Salt water made his eyes painful. His ears were ringing. A gash on his right hand had turned a hideous colour. Because he had swallowed oil, bouts of diarrhoea followed. Also, he was not really swimming, just lying on his back. Despair was taking hold.

An American ship-based floatplane was flying nearby. He expected the rat-tat-tat of a machine gun. It did not come. Instead, the plane must have indicated his position, for now he saw a small landing craft heading towards him. To his horror he realized that there was nowhere to hide. He could not even disappear under the water. He had tried that. Now he was feeling as helpless as a mouse being eyed by a cat. The landing craft came closer. Two American sailors reached down to pick him up. 'No thanks,' he blurted out in English. Even though he struggled and tried to resist, they heaved him on board.

So Michiharu Shinya became a prisoner of war. He was landed on a part of Guadalcanal held by the Americans, and put in a compound with other men from *Akatsuki*. During the first few days of captivity, several men from the lost destroyer died. Shinya himself made a pitiful spectacle, lying on the ground with his light-brown uniform covered in oil, with raw, open wounds and in a totally dazed stupor.

In the Japanese armed forces at that time, it was considered a disgrace to be captured. Men like Shinya were convinced that it was better to die than become a prisoner. As he lay in a tent he was convinced that he did not deserve medical treatment. On the contrary, he believed that he deserved death. Flies swarmed onto his open wounds. His ears throbbed and oozed pus. His mental state was worse. It was as if an accusing voice blamed him for not fighting with more determination. Though confused, his stressed mind turned over and over seeking a way to regain honour. He kept thinking of ways he could arrange to die. Sometimes he would think about the shell that killed the other men on the bridge. Why had he not died with them? It was strange that even his assistant, who was standing beside him, had died. Why should that happen? When the ship went under, sucking down the captain, the navigating officer and himself, why had only one of them floated up again?

He envied the dead. He fantasized about having a pistol and shooting himself. There was always the possibility that his injuries might take his life. The pus coming from his ears gave hope that something serious might be wrong. Days were spent motionless. Outwardly an observer might have said he looked peaceful; inside a storm was raging.

Michiharu Shinya's next destination was New Caledonia, a French colonial island in the Pacific to the east of Australia—even further away from Japanese forces. On board the transport ship the prisoners were given a compulsory shower. That cleared the oil from his body. Still absorbed by thoughts about dying, he had eaten almost nothing. When questioned, he told lies. To hide his shame at being a prisoner, he invented a name for himself, Masaharu Kawai. If news reached Japan about prisoners, it would save his family from ostracism. In fact the authorities informed his family that he had been killed in action.

Shinya's mental struggle with the supposed 'disgrace' of being a prisoner is explained by the indoctrination he had received in early life. The Japanese government, a military dictatorship, portrayed death in battle as an honour. It was all part of the wicked system that instilled into a whole generation the racist belief that the Japanese were superior to decadent Europeans and Americans. This in turn led to terrible atrocities among helpless prisoners captured by the Japanese. Almost all these men and women were treated with contempt, and tortured in the most hideous and disgusting ways.

In New Caledonia Shinya was forcibly put into an ambulance. A doctor at a field hospital treated his ears and dressed his wounds.

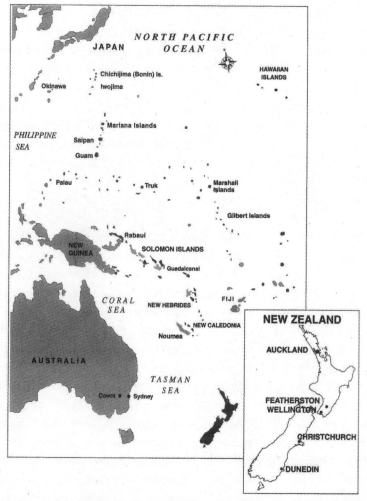

Map showing the chief places mentioned in the story of Michiharu Shinya

About this time his determination to die lessened. The instinct for survival and life asserted itself. Though he knew he was being treated with kindness, he still had hostile feelings towards the 'enemy', and stubbornly refused to speak to, or thank them.

Christmas 1942 saw him still in hospital, but feeling much better. The nurses brought Christmas presents supplied by the Australian Red Cross. He had never heard of 'Christmas' and had no idea why he should be given a well-cooked turkey dinner. There were celebrations and singing, but his dominant emotion was one of resentment. He felt misery at being treated with natural human kindness.

It was now January 1943. High summer brought clear and bright skies, but no amount of sunshine could remove the dark feelings of disgrace. An American officer informed him that he would be sent to New Zealand. He was taken to a merchant ship for the journey. On the voyage he speculated about what this country would be like. Guards from the New Zealand Army took over from the Americans at the city of Auckland. The prisoners began a long train journey across the North Island. Eventually, they stopped at a small country town called Featherston. Not far to the east was the prisoner-of-war camp, built on an open plain. As he entered the camp, a crowd of unhappy Japanese watched. Shinya was startled to find that the enemy had so many prisoners.

Featherston camp already held at least 400 Japanese prisoners who had been captured while working on the construction of Guadalcanal airfield. Other prisoners of war from the Japanese Army, Navy and Air Force brought the total to nearly 800. Outwardly, all was calm, but Shinya soon discovered that there was a hard core of violent men determined to cause trouble. In fact, plans were afoot for a riot. Matters reached boiling point on 25 February 1943. A warning shot was fired, as around 250 Japanese grew angry and started throwing stones. The armed guard of about thirty men opened fire when the enraged Japanese tried to rush them. When the firing stopped forty-eight Japanese were dead and an estimated seventy-four wounded. One New Zealander was hit and killed by a ricocheting bullet. Shinya, who was in a different compound, heard the firing but could do nothing.

Even after such an incident, Featherston camp soon settled down to dull monotony. The injured Japanese were treated well in hospital. The majority abandoned thoughts of further resistance. All Shinya had to do was eat three meals a day, smoke and play cards. Boredom with prison routine gave him time for reflection. How were the members of his family? In his mind he pictured his father, who was a civil servant in the city of Tokyo water department, going to work each day. He also wondered about his two older sisters and his younger brother. What would they be doing right now?

In his mind he went over his life up till now. Born in 1920, he had always been fascinated by the sea and ships, ever since he was a boy. On leaving school, he had gone straight into the Japanese Naval Academy at Etajima (1937–1940). Promotion in the navy came quickly. The early naval battles in which he took part at the Aleutian Islands, Malaya and Sumatra had been easy victories for the Japanese. The ease of the early triumphs had induced a light-hearted mood when going into battle. All that ended when his ship, *Akatsuki*, had been sunk, and he found himself in this boring camp at Featherston.

Shortly after the riot, Dr Bossard, the Swiss delegate of the International Red Cross, visited the camp on a tour of inspection. He mentioned in his report that he had been surprised to receive a request from some Japanese prisoners 'for spiritual advice in connection with the Christian faith'. Dr Bossard added, 'These men are not Christians but want to understand our way of life.'

In May 1943 this unusual request reached the desk of the colonel in charge of New Zealand military forces in the area. The colonel wrote a letter to the Rev. Hessell Troughton, whose Presbyterian church was nearby. The colonel had done his homework. Aged twenty-seven, Troughton had gone to Japan in 1934 as a missionary with the Central Japan Pioneer Mission. Tensions within Japan eventually led to his being shadowed and harassed by the military police. In December 1939, Troughton and his wife Alison left Japan and returned to church work in their native New Zealand.

In Featherston camp Shinya heard the news: a military chaplain who could speak the Japanese language had been appointed. Shinya took the usual view of the Japanese that Christianity was a European/ American religion: 'My mind was firmly made up that even if this chaplain did come, I would have absolutely nothing to do with Christianity.' Shinya had been brought up as a Buddhist, though the family was not strict in its observances. If he believed in anything, it was in the rightness of Japan's military government and the wars it had instigated.

In August 1943, at the height of winter Captain Troughton began to hold weekly meetings in the camp. He brought with him a Japanese Bible and left it in the recreation hut. Among the Japanese officers there was scorn for those who attended Bible studies. Shinya was one of the critics. He wrote, 'No blue-eyed, red-headed foreign missionary would be allowed to tie down my thoughts.'

Keith Robertson, an interpreter for the officers in Featherston, had also done church mission work in Japan. He brought several dozen books in Japanese. They were on a variety of subjects. Shinya looked through them. One caught his eye. It was an article called 'Sorrow in Victory' written by Roka Tokutomi. Mostly to fill in time, he read it. It was the text of an address given to Japanese high-school students shortly after the Japanese victory over Tsarist Russia in 1905. Basically, it questioned the worship of strength and the ultimate value of war. Since life is short, Roka urged the students to think about spiritual matters. The final paragraph read: 'Gentlemen, those who live with the Spirit will never die. As I step down from this platform, I shall conclude by quoting the words spoken by a Hebrew prophet: "Those who hope in the Lord will renew their strength. They shall soar on wings like eagles; they will run and not grow weary; they will walk and not be faint."'

The article proved a turning point. As Roka suggested, Shinya decided to seek the truth. Concerning that last sentence, quoted from the Hebrew prophet, Shinya later wrote, 'It burnt a deep mark in my heart, and possessed the power to draw my spirit.'

It was now September 1943. Shinya's first decision was to

Pastor Hessell Troughton in the uniform of a New Zealand army chaplain

find the words Roka had quoted. He guessed that they would probably be in the Old Testament. That meant he would need Padre Troughton's Bible after all. Having plenty of time, he decided to read at least until he found the words from the Hebrew prophet. He started at the first page of Genesis, then Exodus, Leviticus and in sequence through the Bible.

Through the reading he entered a new world—the world of the Bible. While other men grew fruit and vegetables, Shinya read the Bible. He read the books of Samuel, Kings, Job and Psalms. Still there was no sign of the words Roka had quoted.

On 13 November 1943 he had been a prisoner for one full year. Dr Bossard had arranged for *Hawaii Times* printed in Japanese to be delivered to Featherston. Magazines such as *Life* were allowed and local newspapers were smuggled in. As a result the prisoners knew the latest news. As the Allied forces grew stronger, the camp authorities became more tolerant. While the war raged all over the world, Shinya continued his search. He reached a prophet called Isaiah. 'It was the first time in my life that I had ever encountered such a book, or writings of such splendid power. Then I read chapter 40, and right at the end I found those words which had been my goal':

> ... those who hope in the LORD
>   will renew their strength.
> They will soar on wings like eagles;
>   they will run and not grow weary,
>   they will walk and not be faint
>
>   (Isaiah 40:31).

These were the words that led him to the Bible; but where would the Bible lead him? He later commented: 'No one forgets the first words they knew from the Bible. As long as I live I shall not forget the text which first led me there.' Boosted by his discovery, he finished the Old Testament and read on into the New Testament.

Christmas 1943 came. In the southern hemisphere, spring had slipped into summer. Padre Troughton and others brought presents, and there was plenty of ice cream available. The New Zealanders seemed happy. However, to Shinya jokes and laughter were hollow. The news of the war was bad. At night when he stepped out of his hut to gaze at the grandeur of the stars in the jet-black night sky, human affairs seemed so trivial in comparison with the immensity of the universe above him. Trapped in this obscure place, he felt cut off from the real world. He was a creature cast aside from real events. The sheep grazing peacefully beyond the barbed wire were freer than he was.

When 1944 arrived, his Bible-reading flagged. He had started with a flourishing spirit of enquiry. Now he was a little tired and was finding all reading hard going. Parts of the Bible were hard to understand. The stories of the miracles were incomprehensible to human reason. He gave up in favour of billiards.

March and April 1944 brought autumn. Diagnosed as suffering from malaria, Shinya was removed to hospital and treated with quinine. A week later his friend Junior Lieutenant Hirahashi visited him, bringing reading materials. Among them was a booklet called *The Reason Why*. Robert Laidlaw, who owned the biggest department store in New Zealand, had written this simple outline of how to become a Christian, originally to explain his beliefs to his staff. Thirty-three million copies in thirty languages would eventually be printed. It challenged Shinya. He wrote, 'I was driven to the brink of either believing or not believing in Jesus Christ.'

Earlier he had read the New Testament without faith. Now it was different. His heart and mind were convinced that only faith in an absolute God made sense of the otherwise meaningless human condition. His spiritual struggles all related to the surrender of his life to Jesus Christ. The gospel demanded repentance and faith, but his ego, his self, his pride, prevented him from surrendering again, surrendering his life to Jesus Christ.

One day Padre Troughton visited him. Up to this point Shinya had not liked to be seen talking to him too much. The chaplain had the right words for the situation. 'He spoke briefly about salvation through Jesus Christ. His voice was quiet but carried a powerful conviction, and I felt an authority that was hard to defy. It was not just the Padre speaking but, more than that, through the Padre I felt as though Jesus Christ was living and beginning to speak to me directly.'

The treatment for malaria was successful. After two weeks he was discharged from hospital. A few days later, on 12 May 1944, a Bible-study meeting was held in the compound. From that day the twenty-four-year-old Michiharu Shinya began to attend these meetings regularly. Concerning this he wrote:

> This day became a milestone for me, for I decided that the path of Jesus Christ was my life's path, and I chose to follow it. There was no special thing about the proceedings of that meeting itself, but I felt as though a great load had been dropped from my shoulders, and felt some indefinable sense of gladness.

> Complete freedom now ruled my life. There in the camp, with its apparent restrictions and lack of freedom, I now came to experience complete freedom though faith in Jesus Christ. It could be said that only the external restraint of the prison camp fences brought the opportunity for true internal freedom. In this way a POW camp changed into a unique paradise on earth. That is no exaggerated statement. An entirely new life opened up there.

> Five months after that epoch-making day that clearly divided my life into two [on 6 October 1944], several of us were baptized by Padre Troughton. I remember how the Padre put water into a red-lacquered wooden bowl which he had brought back with him from Japan, and how, after saying some words, he dipped his hand in the water, and laid that hand on my head. I felt glad that with this I had clearly become identified as one of Christ's people. Now that I had been distinctly marked before all men, I felt that there could be no drawing back.

> After this there was the celebration of Holy Communion. It was my first time with this ceremony, involving the eating

of a finely cut piece of bread and the drinking of a minute quantity of grape wine.

I was no longer bewitched by that beautiful word 'patriotism'. How ignorant and blind we Japanese had been until now! I myself had loved Japan without limit. I had burned with an ardent desire to show my love in some way. For this very reason I had enrolled in the Naval Academy, hoping for a chance to do my best for our country. My patriotism and that of others had expressed itself in conceited and madly mistaken beliefs. We had believed that Japan was the indestructible and invincible land of the gods, that the Emperor was a god present as man, and that Japan was the centre of the universe. It had taken me so long to realize the error of these things.

There could hardly have been a greater contrast. Outside of Featherston camp, the world was in tumult. Inside it, Shinya and a few other officers had weekly meetings for Bible study. The group would gather round the ping-pong table with their books and papers, sing hymns together and listen to talks about the Bible by the padre. Shinya recalled that Troughton often said, 'A person who has been saved should pass it on to others also.' The padre's voice was never far from his inner ear. Shinya accepted that the faith he had been given brought him inward joy and an assurance of sins forgiven through the cross of Jesus Christ. He had a personal relationship with God himself that would persist beyond death. There was not much need to convince him that it was important to be a witness.

Shinya had a good grasp of English, having been taught it at middle school and at Etajima Naval Academy. After praying in secret about how to be a witness, he decided to translate a book from Japanese to English. Toyohiko Kagawa's book *Christ and Japan*

The group that met for Bible study under the leadership of Captain Troughton. Michiharu Shinya is second from left in the front row.

was available, so he set about translating it. He then circulated his translation as widely as he was able.

The Japanese Christian officers asked Troughton for a deeper study of the Bible in order to understand the biblical message in a systematic, joined-up way. He procured a suitable study book from the Bible College of New Zealand. The other officers selected Shinya as their leader. He was asked to translate each study and present a talk on what it said. Plainly, his intellectual leadership qualities were evident to his comrades.

Christmas 1944 was his second Christmas at Featherston and his third as a prisoner. The prisoners received greetings from members of Troughton's church. Mrs Troughton sent a cake. All this reminded them that the man they knew as military chaplain had another sphere of work in his local church that was demanding, and full-time. It was a hot day and once again they had ice cream. Of all the gifts he received, the one he valued most was 'the boundless and deep grace and peace of God in the Lord Jesus Christ'.

The new year brought him a new self-imposed task. One of the guards who was a Christian lent Shinya a book by Scotsman Henry Drummond called *The Greatest Thing in the World*. One day, as he was translating it into Japanese, sirens and bells filled the air. Hitler and his Nazi state had vanished from the face of the earth. The local New Zealanders were celebrating, as well they might.

Through the efforts of Dr Bossard of the Red Cross, the prisoners were now allowed to see films once a fortnight. One of those seen by Shinya was about British cities of learning such as Edinburgh and Cambridge. He felt a burning desire for scholarship. It seemed as if the world of learning beckoned him after the war ended.

On 15 August 1945 the noise of sirens sounded jubilantly again. The Allies were victorious. The war in the Pacific was over. The Japanese military junta had surrendered. Now the world could start to come back to life.

Shinya recorded his plans: 'I greatly wished to study the Bible, and if possible enrol in a theological college ... as far as I was now concerned there could be no other path in life. This was because I understood only too well that if I could not live for Jesus Christ and him alone, there would be in the end no value in trying to live in any other way.'

He was particularly attracted to the Old Testament. It was the first part of the Bible he had read. Now he was reading it again. One thing that made a great impression on him was the explanation of history: 'What I saw there was an account of humanity's struggles, its ceaseless wars. Human history is certainly no history of peace. From just knowing this, any optimistic view of mankind should be corrected. What the Old Testament shows lies deeper. I grasped that the cause of these wars is to be sought in the relationship between man and God. It always comes back to the fact that mankind does not know the living and true God. There is a state of rebellion against God. In other words, the reality of human sin is the cause of wars. I felt I had been shown the ultimate problem of mankind. What we had previously been taught as history was in the main no more than a history of governments and the recital of historical incidents. The problem lay more deeply, within human beings themselves. So the Old Testament became very close and dear to me. It spanned the gap of the centuries.' His conviction was that the Old Testament prophets pointed to the Christ who was to come.

Always a thoughtful man, Shinya wanted to know why only a few of his fellow Japanese became Christians. It was obviously nothing to do with intellectual ability, since the most unlearned person could exercise simple faith in Christ. One of the most offensive features of the biblical faith to the men was the blunt assertion that all men are sinners needing redemption. Many prisoners were very indignant to learn that the Bible labelled them as sinners. Shinya wrote, 'People are attached to a mistaken overconfidence in human nature, and to their own pride. When we realize how deeply-rooted and stubborn this is, we see how difficult it is for people to accept a belief based on the Bible.' In this way the prisoners were really little different in their reaction from most people who hear the gospel. To the end only a handful of men believed in Christ. The majority believed that they were not sinners in God's sight, preferring their own way, not that of Christ and the Bible.

On 30 December 1945 the prisoners left Featherston on the first leg of their homeward journey. To the end, the Christian group kept up its weekly meetings with Padre Troughton. Just over three years had passed since *Akatsuki* had sunk. Though sad about the horror of the war, Shinya was happy that he had come into contact with the world of the Bible. He had been touched by the gospel of the cross of Christ: 'I felt only deep gratitude towards

*The prisoners leave Featherston Camp bound for Japan
on 30 December 1945.*

God's boundless grace and love as shown in the cross of Christ ...
I had been granted freedom from the guilt of sin and a personal
relationship with God through repentance and faith in Christ. I
had been reborn spiritually.'

Troughton gave them a cheerful farewell at Wellington,
suggesting they should read Psalm 27 on the ship. The first leg of
the journey took them to Guadalcanal. That port of call evoked a
flood of mixed memories.

Two months later, on 3 February 1946, and now aged twenty-
five, Shinya reached the land of his birth. Would his family have
survived the bombing? Was it his turn to be sad? Fortunately,
they had all survived, but they had said funeral rites for him! It
was like the homecoming of a ghost. The Japanese sailor who had
given the wrong name through shame had returned with a new
life, a new belief and a new vision. He was welcomed with joy and
was particularly relieved that none of his family showed hostility
towards him on account of his conversion to Christianity.

As Shinya looked at the ruins of his country, he recognized that his wartime experiences had not taken away the love of Japan. But from now on that love would be wiser and never unthinking.

Now came the big test. Would the influences of the prison camp wear off as he settled back into post-war Japan? Or would he stick to his spiritual vision?

Two months after his return the opportunity opened up for him to enrol at the newly founded Japan Biblical Seminary in Tokyo. Three years of study followed. 1949 was marked not only by his graduation, but by his marriage to Junko. They later had two sons and a daughter. Then he served for four years as minister of a church in Kanuma City, Tochigi Prefecture.

In addition to the continual round of preaching and pastoral work, he prepared articles for his church bulletin entitled 'From a Destroyer to the Pulpit'. These became the basis of his book of testimony, *Beyond Death and Dishonour*. The idea for this book goes back to the days when Shinya was a young theology student after the war. He needed to learn Greek to gain an accurate understanding of the original language of the New Testament. On one occasion his Greek teacher, Toshiro Suzuki, mentioned how Pastor Martin Niemöller had written in his life-story about how he had commanded a German submarine while in the navy. This gave Shinya the idea of writing his own story one day.

Having passed an examination, he was given the opportunity to study in the United States. After four years at McCormick Theological Seminary in Chicago, he graduated as Master of Theology. While in Chicago, he often preached in local Japanese Presbyterian churches.

In April 1958 Shinya returned from America to serve at the Japan Biblical Seminary as Professor of Old Testament. It was a strategic setting, training young men for Christian service. In 1973 his abilities were recognized once more when he became principal of the seminary. Concurrently, he was pastor of the Akebono

Church in the western part of Tokyo. He published commentaries on the Old Testament books of Deuteronomy and Chronicles, as well as translating other Christian books into Japanese. He retired from his position as principal in 1987, aged sixty-seven. He did not finally retire from church ministry until March 1996, when he was seventy-six.

In 1980 he revisited the now derelict site of Featherston camp. New Zealand television produced a programme about him in the course of which he remarked, 'The first time I came to New Zealand as a prisoner of war. This time I come as a prisoner of Jesus Christ.'

In 1992 Robert D. Ballard, the underwater researcher who found the remains of the *Titanic,* invited Shinya to join the search for sunken ships in the waters near Guadalcanal. There are nearly eighty wrecks in the area. As a result the former battle zone where *Akatsuki* now lies is marked on some maps as 'Iron Bottom Sound'. The subsequent book, *The Lost Ships of Guadalcanal,* is the record of the expedition. Many ships lost in the battles for Guadalcanal were found, but not *Akatsuki.*

In the 2001 edition of *Beyond Death and Dishonour*, Shinya included a personal statement called 'Epilogue to the Wounded', in which he pays tribute to the good treatment given

Mr and Mrs Shinya in Yokohama, 2000

to Japanese prisoners by the Allies. In contrast he apologizes for the well-documented atrocities committed by his fellow countrymen against the prisoners of Japan.

Over sixty years after its sinking Shinya still keeps an accurate model of *Akatsuki* in his living room. He has never lost contact with his wartime naval friends, or the New Zealanders who gave him so much.

When he was eighty-four the writer put the following question to him in an email: 'What is the most important event in your long life?' To that he answered: 'For me the experience of my conversion and new birth in Jesus Christ while a prisoner of war at Featherston was so strong that I wished to dedicate all my life to his service.'

Asked whether the Bible was still as important as it had been while he was at Featherston, Michiharu Shinya replied, 'Every morning I read three chapters of different parts of the Bible, and every year I read through the whole book.'[1]

More information on Michiharu Shinya

The first time I heard of Michiharu Shinya was in 1980. He had just revisited Featherston prisoner-of-war camp, and the Bible Society newspaper *Word in Action* reported the event in the Autumn 1980 issue.

His book called *The Path from Guadalcanal* (first published in 1979) was supplied to me by its translator Eric Thompson in 1982. Thompson, who spoke Japanese, was a guard there. Eric Thompson's translation was not marketed well, and he was left with many copies. Castle Publishing, Auckland, New Zealand, republished the story as *Beyond Death and Dishonour*. Kay Wall revised the text, using up-to-date English.

Thanks are due to Andrew Killick for supplying Mr Shinya's email address. That led to more emails than I can count from Mr Shinya, who was eighty-five years old at the time. With the extra information supplied by Mr Shinya, his story really 'lives'.

Mrs Doreen Payne supplied information and a photograph of her father, Hessell Troughton. I record my gratitude for her help.

Pastor Hessell Troughton's Presbyterian background probably had a deep influence on Michiharu Shinya. In an email to the author, Shinya calls his basic beliefs 'Presbyterian', and in an interview recorded in New Zealand he describes his conversion and Christian life in a totally God-centred way, consistent with the theological beliefs that undergird his book.

It is my hope that readers will want to read *Beyond Death and Dishonour* for themselves. At any level, it is an outstanding book and is one of the very few memoirs written by a Japanese veteran.

12

Werner Simonson

German judge and Anglican minister

The moment the Nazis found out his racial background, the fact that he had fought for Germany and had won the coveted Iron Cross for gallantry counted for nothing. His career as a judge was over. He was sacked there and then.

Werner Simonson

12

Werner Simonson[1]

I t was October 1914. The First World War had just started. On the western front French and German armies were already locked in fierce battles. Werner Simonson was one of a group of fifty German soldiers from the 4th Guards regiment involved in the Battle of Diksmuide in Belgium. They had just taken prisoner over thirty French soldiers. The man Simonson had captured had been a schoolmaster before being called up. He seemed particularly distressed at the turn of events, so Simonson spoke kindly to him in French and shared some of his rations with the unhappy man.

As daylight came and the early morning mist cleared, the fifty German soldiers, with their prisoners, found that they were trapped between two French trenches. The French immediately opened fire. Within a few minutes most of the Germans were killed or wounded. The two officers in charge of the Germans, a major and a captain, were killed right next to Simonson. He survived by lying down in a small hollow in the ground. The firing stopped. Fifteen Germans remained alive.

The French now came out of their trenches to deal with the

fifteen Germans who were left. In a victorious mood, the French took their prisoners. Then the attitude of the victors changed dramatically. The French were outraged to discover that some of the Frenchmen previously captured by the Germans had been killed in the confusion. The Germans were wrongly accused of having shot them deliberately. As a reprisal, five Germans, including Simonson, were lined up for execution.

Just as the French officer was about to shout, 'Fire!', the former schoolmaster came forward and said something to the officer in charge of the firing party. As a result, Simonson and one other German were led away and saved from death. The other three German soldiers were shot. The schoolmaster who had saved Simonson's life did not even wait around to be thanked.

Werner Simonson recorded this story in his memoirs to show the importance of small acts of kindness. In later life he became known for them. He realized how often very small things can have unforeseen effects, either for good or evil. What he did *not* record was that he was awarded the Iron Cross. It was given for the bravery and good conduct he displayed during the fighting in Flanders.

During that comparatively minor battle two thirds of Simonson's battalion were killed in a single night. Most were young students from Berlin. Whenever Simonson subsequently referred to the Battle of Diksmuide, he called it the 'slaughter of Berlin's youth'.

So Werner Simonson became a prisoner of the French. He was not to know that his imprisonment would last for over five long years. Considering the enormous casualty figures among infantry soldiers on both sides in the First World War, his capture may well have saved his life. For most of the time he was forced to work on farms in the south of France. Even though he was not treated cruelly, he found life as a prisoner both hard and tedious.

He longed to see his father, mother and two sisters—Ilse, the eldest, and Maggie, who was younger. His father was an important Supreme Court judge in Berlin. Werner had been brought up in an atmosphere of high culture, appreciating music, painting and an aristocratic lifestyle. If only he could go home and resume his university studies to be a lawyer!

He now began to believe that he had given these studies up too quickly in the excitement of the early months of the war. Knowing only what the censored German newspapers told them, he and his friends had rushed to join the army in case the war ended before

Werner Simonson photographed while a prisoner in France, 1914–20

they had a chance to fight. They had been given six weeks of hurried training. Then they were issued with new grey uniforms and put on a train heading for Belgium and France. Somebody painted the words, 'Holiday train to Paris,' on the carriages packed with high-spirited German soldiers. He felt proud when civilians threw sweets and cigarettes to the departing troops. Enthusiastic crowds cheered them on their way to what seemed inevitable triumph. He recalled seeing a 'victory' parade in Berlin with large quantities of guns and military equipment that had been captured on the Russian front. Deep down he had the unpleasant feeling that it would have been better to wait until victory really was won.

He had suppressed such thoughts at the time, carried along by enthusiastic propaganda and patriotism.

If only he had not believed the Kaiser when he claimed falsely that Germany was being attacked! He thought about the Kaiser's boast that he would eat his Christmas dinner in Buckingham Palace. Being a prisoner gave Simonson a different perspective. It all seemed so empty now.

The world suffered a disastrous influenza epidemic during 1918 and 1919. Millions died from what the newspapers called 'Spanish flu'. Six million people died in India, and tens of thousands in most other countries. More United States soldiers in Europe lost their lives because of influenza than were killed in action by the enemy. Simonson was struck down by it in the autumn of 1918, and was fortunate to survive. The family of the French farmer for whom he was working nursed him back to health. Even though he was one of the 'enemy', he was treated as part of the family. Nevertheless, many captive Germans and French villagers perished because of the flu epidemic. Understandably, not all German prisoners were treated as kindly as he was.

At 11.00 on a grey November morning in 1918, he was working in the fields of Provence as usual, when the bells of the village church began to peal. He could also hear the bells of churches in surrounding villages. The First World War was over. The bloodshed had ended at last. The unconfined joy of the French was matched by the misery of the Germans who knew that they were defeated. News came through that the Kaiser had fled to neutral Holland seeking asylum.

At first Simonson and his friends thought that release would soon follow. In April 1919 they were escorted to a train. The German prisoners were excited. Surely this train would take them home? Slowly the train made its way from the beautiful Mediterranean coast to the north of France. After Dijon, it travelled through areas devastated by the war. From the window

Simonson could see houses in ruins, trees cut down and fields laid waste. Then came disappointment. They would not be going home. They were split into groups to help with the restoration of the war-torn areas. It was not until early 1920 that Simonson was eventually released.

At the time, he thought his five years in captivity were completely wasted. Later on he changed his mind. As life unfolded, he realized that he had learned lessons that moulded his character and taught him how to cope with difficult situations. In his words, 'We all had to live together in conditions of hardship, accept our limitations and renounce any notions of self-importance.' No experience in life is wasted, he concluded.

Simonson returned to his family in Leipzig, arriving late one night. Naturally, they wept with joy and surprise. Before many days had passed he noticed the obvious: he had come back to a land that was totally different from the one he had left more than five years earlier. People were bitter and disunited by the defeat. His father, who was an ardent monarchist, was greatly upset by the change from the autocratic Kaiser to a republican democracy. Germany was engulfed in political strife. Even in the streets of Leipzig there was totally unexpected shooting. There were also disturbances in many other German towns. Political parties accused one another of being responsible for the nation's debacle in the recent war.

After a few weeks of recuperation, Simonson plunged into his interrupted university studies. He was a man with considerable ability. As a result, his progress was rapid. In 1921, at the age of thirty-one, he passed the examinations to become Doctor of Law. In 1925 he was appointed as a judge. By 1928 he was a high-court judge presiding over commercial law cases. Although qualified in both criminal and civil law, he always preferred dealing with civil cases. His income was increased by writings for legal periodicals.

His name became well known in legal circles because of his authoritative contributions to a lawyers' yearbook.

During this period of success and advancement, he married Leonie in July 1923. She too had an aristocratic background. Their only child, a son called Juergen, was born in 1924. Considerable financial security enabled them to travel and enjoy excellent holidays every year in the most luxurious surroundings—such as the Bavarian Alps, the Tyrol, Lake Lucerne, Zermatt and the Dolomites. There were few limits on their pleasures.

The Simonsons' circumstances were so comfortable that their way of life appeared to be unaffected by Germany's economic problems. From 1919 to 1933 Germany was ruled by a parliament called the National Assembly. This held its meetings at Weimar because Berlin was torn by political unrest. As a result the government became known as the Weimar Republic. The politicians had no experience of democracy, and Germany was in virtually constant political and economic turmoil.

Most Germans felt frustrated by the Treaty of Versailles that had been imposed on their delegates in Paris at the end of the war. A large number believed that Germany had been treated unfairly. People were ready to believe the myth that Germany had been 'stabbed in the back' by the Jews and other traitors, and that the German army had not been beaten on the battlefield. Ordinary people did not feel that they had been beaten because the Allies had never occupied the country as conquerors. Dr Simonson was not particularly interested in these things. He did not like the instability in his country, but he made no attempt to change the direction of public affairs. Law was his sphere, not politics.

In 1933 Adolf Hitler was legally appointed Chancellor of Germany. On the day he took office a friend remarked to Simonson, 'This is the end of Germany's freedom. In future the Nazis will suppress all other views.' Before long this was proved correct. All political groups other than the Nazi party

Werner and Leonie Simonson on their wedding day, 16 July 1923.
Although Werner was clearly proud to wear his Iron Cross on that
occasion, in his memoir the Iron Cross is not even mentioned.

were abolished. The parliament building was burnt down. Hitler became a dictator with all the levers of power in his control. At the end of March 1933 Simonson heard a radio broadcast by Hitler's propaganda minister and leading spokesman, Goebbels. In it he called the Jews 'sub-human monkeys' and 'the dregs of society'. Then came the news that the great Jewish conductor Bruno Walter had been forbidden to give a concert.

Windows of businesses owned by Jews were smashed. No Jew was allowed to hold public office. Because of this ruling, Nazi leaders went to all places of employment asking if there were any Jews working there. They interviewed Werner Simonson and found out that, although his parents had converted to Christianity and been baptized as Lutherans, all four of his grandparents were Jewish. Therefore, by race Simonson and his parents were Jewish, though they had no connections with any Jewish people.

The moment the Nazis found out his racial background, the fact that he had fought for Germany and had won the coveted Iron Cross for gallantry counted for nothing. His career as a judge was over. He was sacked there and then. That happened just as he was on the verge of appointment to a very senior job in the legal profession—judge in an appeal court.

Shortly afterwards, Simonson received letters from his publishers saying that, for obvious reasons, they were no longer able to publish books he had written. One of his works, a legal commentary, was even published under a false name. Overnight he became an outcast. People who had been eager to visit the family because of his social position now changed their minds. Some would walk on the other side of the street to avoid meeting him. It saddened him that highly educated people were quickly influenced by this prejudice. But as he said, 'We learned who were our real friends.'

All his advantages vanished. He could not obtain work of any kind. Even the boys in his son's class at school wrote on the blackboard, 'We do not want a Jew in our form; the Jew must go.' Simonson's passport had a huge 'J' (for 'Jew') stamped on it. Theatres and hotels put up notices saying, 'No admission to Jews.'

In 1938, under the strain of waiting to be arrested, Simonson's health broke down. He had a heart attack and a nervous breakdown. The first doctor who was called refused to see him because Simonson was 'Jewish'. Eventually, his friend Dr Schmoeger treated him, at the risk of losing his own job.

In the same year, when he was forty-nine years old, Simonson had an experience that was to change his life. In a gloomy mood, he went to Dresden to visit his married sister Maggie and her family. It was his niece's confirmation service. This involved attendance at a local Lutheran church. At the time Werner Simonson thought Greek philosophy was more important than the Christian faith. He believed that the philosopher Socrates was a greater man than Jesus. Why? His explanation was that 'Jesus had died expecting to rise again, but Socrates had given his life for his convictions without expecting any reward. I did not believe in a personal God, nor in a personal relationship with God through faith in Jesus.'

During the service the

Front page of Werner Simonson's passport, showing the large 'J' for 'Jew'. Note also the addition of the name 'Israel' to his three genuine first names.

preacher spoke about some men who need to reach a kind of abyss, when they can go neither forward nor back, where they are completely at the end of all hope, before they can discover the way to God. Simonson wrote, 'He pictured this situation so vividly, as though he knew exactly my state of mind, my frustration, and was preaching just for me. It was as if God spoke to me and called me by name, as if he said, "I have a new way for you, a new life, if you will respond to my call." It was like a revelation to me.'

He could not resist God's call. 'In the utter darkness which had engulfed my life I saw a new light. I met God, not only as the God of nature, not as the unapproachable God, far too great to be accessible to man, but now as a personal God in a "You—I" relationship, as a completely new experience. He in his mercy had revealed himself to me through the preacher's words. God had touched my heart. It was more than an emotional effect.' It was the beginning of a new era in his life.

He returned to his wife and son with a new hope and with faith in his heart. Praying, reading the Bible and going to church with his family became regular parts of his life. The church was in a small village near Forst, south of Berlin. It was Lutheran, and its leader, Pastor Jacob, preached only from the Bible and supported the Confessing Church. Simonson's ideas began to change. He recorded: 'From the Gospels I saw that my ideas about Jesus were wrong. I came to the conclusion that either Jesus was the Son of God, as he had claimed to be, or he was a deceiver or self-deceived. No Old Testament prophets had dared to forgive sins, because they knew that God alone could do it. Jesus forgave sin. The prophets spoke in the name of God. Jesus said, "I am the way, and the truth, and the life. No one comes to the Father except through me"; "I am the light of the world"; "I am the bread of life"; "I am the good shepherd"; "I am the door"; "I am the resurrection and the life"; "I and the Father are one"; "Before Abraham was I am."'

Werner Simonson began to understand for the first time that Jesus' death on the cross was 'God's act of love, his power to overrule man's will, forgiving sin, and drawing people to the Father'. He wrote, 'We cannot come to God in our own strength, or by what we do, but by what Jesus has done to forgive sin by faith in him. The more I read the Bible, the more God's Spirit entered into me. Through God I came to Christ and in Jesus I found the truth of God. In this connection, another thought came to me: if the gospel is not true, if God does not exist, then human life is accidental, without purpose and not worth living.'

He came to believe that godlessness was one of the causes of Nazism in Germany, a country so long full of criticism of the Bible. Simonson's memoir says, 'The evil in this world results from man's separation from God. It is not the fault of God.'

He was now not only a marked man because he was 'Jewish', but because he associated with the Confessing Church, composed of both Lutherans and Reformed Christians, all of whom openly opposed Hitler. Members of the Confessing Church particularly rejected those who called themselves 'German Christians' for adopting Nazi beliefs. Simonson knew that the cross had been removed from some of these 'churches' and replaced by a picture of Hitler. The Nazis had appointed one of this group, Mueller, as a bishop, with the aim of controlling the 'German Christians'.

It would only be a matter of time before the Gestapo, the state secret police, arrested Simonson. His wife was safe because she was not Jewish in any way. One woman asked his wife why he didn't commit suicide to make life easier for her! Leonie started to urge him strongly to escape from Germany.

With the help of Dr George Bell, Bishop of Chichester, and other English friends, Simonson obtained a visa from the British consulate. Even with this he had to be interviewed by the Gestapo to procure a passport as an emigrant. He and his wife had to report to a Gestapo building. On entering, non-Jews could walk on the carpet in the centre and sit down. Jews had to stand on the stone floor by the wall until they were called. So his wife was allowed to sit, while he had to stand. Leonie decided she would stand with him. When he was called, it was made clear that if he ever returned from England he would be immediately sent to a concentration camp.

On 7 March 1939, when he was nearly fifty, Simonson arrived in Southampton 'and took a deep breath of freedom'. He could speak only broken English, although he was fluent in French and understood Latin and Greek. The German authorities had only allowed him to take ten marks out of the country (a trifling sum). Though virtually penniless, he had something the Nazis could not take away—his faith in God through Jesus Christ. His plan at this time was to be in a position to support his wife and son, and then send for them.

The clouds on the political horizon darkened. People everywhere in Europe were restless and uneasy. It was evident to most people who were alive at the time that Europe was about to explode into the flames of the Second World War.

The moment that war started, an 'iron curtain' came down between Britain and Germany. Simonson's parents, sister, wife and son were all in Germany. What was he to do? The only possible answer was the one he offered in his memoirs: 'I trusted in God and his guidance.' His English friends understood the predicament in which he found himself. Here was a man cut off from his family through no fault of his own. Most of them shook him by the hand to show him that they cared and understood.

As he grew in grace and understanding, he experienced the Lord's call to serve in the Christian ministry. Travelling in England he found sympathy, kindness and Christian fellowship. As his English improved, he started to study. In 1940 the only college prepared to teach him theology and how to preach was the evangelical Anglican college Ridley Hall in Cambridge. There were no fees to pay. The age gap between him and the other students was significant: most of them could have been his sons. He was well past middle age when converted to faith in Christ and, as with many older converts, he was anxious to make the most of what life was left to him.

Suddenly there came a shock. All Germans in Britain were to be rounded up and interned in case they were spies. With Britain under threat of invasion in 1940, the decision to classify all German nationals was understandable. Simonson was put on a train and taken to a newly built housing estate at Huyton near Liverpool. From there he was shipped to Douglas on the Isle of Man, where hotels had been requisitioned.

It took the British authorities some time to sort out which of their German internees were friendly and innocent. Simonson shared a house with other Christians who had escaped from Germany. He discovered that strict Orthodox Jews occupied the hotel next door. He and his friends had discussions with them. The Jews kept up their rituals based on the law. Simonson recorded: 'They were still waiting for the coming of the Messiah. We knew that the Messiah had come, that Jesus was the fulfilment of the prophecies of the Old Testament. Jesus lived with us and in us. They missed this inner assurance that gave us so much strength during our internment.' There was no place in Judaism for such a personal knowledge of God. As a result of their discussions, several Jews became Christians and were baptized in the hotel by a Lutheran pastor. After six months, Simonson was released and returned to Ridley Hall.

From this time onwards tragic news started to come from Germany. His father had died. His eighty-four-year-old mother was murdered in a concentration camp and his sister Ilse was gassed in Auschwitz. His non-Jewish wife and son, however, were spared, along with his sister Maggie, who was married to a non-Jew. Simonson was devastated. For some days he was overwhelmed by

Ex-German Judge To Be Curate

A former High Court judge in Germany, Dr. Werner Simonson, is shortly to be ordained into the Church of England ministry, and will take up a curacy in Fulham.

A supporter of Niemoller, he found all doors closed to him in Germany, and came to England four years ago.

Through the Church of England Committee for refugees Dr. Simonson has completed a three-year course at Ridley Hall, Cambridge, with a view to entering the Ministry, and he is to be ordained by the Bishop of London.

Fulham Chronicle.

GERMAN JUDGE TO BE CURATE IN LONDON

"Star" Reporter

A FORMER High Court judge in Germany is to be ordained into the Church of England by the Bishop of London, Dr. Fisher, and will shortly take up a curacy at Christ Church, Fulham.

He is Dr. Werner Simonson, who was a strong supporter of Niemoller and lay member of the Confessional Church in Germany. Dr. Simonson has been in this country for three and a half years.

I talked today to Dr. Simonson at a house in the country, where he is staying with friends.

"I am most happy about my ordination," he told me. "I was a judge for nearly twenty years, but three and a half years ago I was dismissed.

"I tried to enter the church there, but they would not have me, so I got in touch with a friend in England—the only friend I had in this country at that time, and he put me in touch with the Bishop of Chichester.

"He helped me in every way, and I was introduced to the Church of England Committee for Refugees. I am here alone, as I had to leave my wife and son in Germany."

Evening Star.

DR. WERNER SIMONSON.
On September 27, at St. Paul's Cathedral, Dr. Werner Simonson, a former High Court Judge in Germany, was ordained into the Church of England Ministry by the Bishop of London. A strong supporter of Niemoller, Dr. Simonson had to leave Germany. He will take up a curacy in Fulham.

Illustrated London News.

Cuttings from English newspapers of the time reporting
Werner Simonson's ordination

darkness and grief. He wrestled with God about it until the Lord's compassion restored the light and joy of his salvation.

In the summer of 1942 his time at Ridley Hall came to an end. Even though he was now fifty-two, the call to the ministry was very strong. But would any English church want a German citizen as its minister? The legal authorities of the Church of England wanted proof that he really was a Doctor of Law since he had no documents. Somebody suggested asking the British Museum. Sure enough, it had a record of his thesis dated 17 March 1921, complete with its full title in German.

On 27 September 1942 Simonson was ordained in St Paul's Cathedral, London. British newspapers were full of the amazing story of a German citizen becoming a Church of England minister in the middle of a very serious war against Germany. A typical headline announced: 'Ex-German Judge to be Curate in London.'

At his first charge, Christ Church, Fulham, he maintained a programme of study and prayer in the mornings and four or five evangelistic visits in an afternoon, or twenty-five to thirty every week. He believed that, to sustain his ministry, it was necessary to study the Word of God daily. 'We need to read God's Word as spiritual food as much as we need our daily bread,' was how he expressed his strong conviction on the matter.

One day he heard the sad news that the son of a church member had been killed while flying in the RAF over Germany. Thinking that they would not want to see a German in their grief, he was prepared to be turned away, but when he visited the home, the father and mother were waiting for him. 'We had a wonderful time of fellowship and prayer together,' Simonson recalled later.

In 1944 Werner Simonson received the exciting news that his son, Juergen, now twenty-one, was still alive. He was being used as a slave labourer by the Nazi Todt organization. However, he survived the ordeal, came to England, became a Christian and, like his father, entered the Church of England ministry.

More joy was to come: Leonie, his wife, was the first German civilian to be allowed into England once the war ended in 1945. She proved to be remarkably calm on finding the husband she had last known as a judge had been 'transformed' into a Christian minister. Two years later Dr and Mrs Simonson became British citizens.

After seven years at Fulham, he became vicar of St Mark's, Dalston, also in London. While at Dalston he was asked to return to Germany. The new democratic West German government was genuinely short of judges who were not contaminated by Nazi ideas. Would he be a judge? If not, would he accept a pension for the post he had held before the Nazis had sacked him? It must have seemed an attractive offer. His income at the time was well below the average. He had no car. A bicycle was used for all his visiting. To Werner Simonson the decision was obvious. 'Had I returned,' he wrote, 'I would have been appointed to a high position in the legal profession, yet I could not consider this offer for a moment. I could not exchange service in the ministry of God for service in administering man-made law; accepting this offer would have meant abandoning God's call to me, and this I could not do.'

At the age of sixty-five, he moved to St Luke's Church, Hampstead, where he stayed for over nine years. There were many Jewish people living in Hampstead and during his ministry there ten Jewish people came to faith in Christ and were baptized by Simonson.

By the time he was nearly seventy he was beginning to find cycling on his pastoral visits tiring, so he invested in a motorcycle. He had it for one day, fell off and went back to the bicycle! At the age of seventy-five he retired and was succeeded by Bible scholar and preacher Rev. Alec Motyer.

Werner Simonson lived to be 101, dying in February 1991. Those who knew him commented on his godliness, prayerfulness and the favourable impression that he made on people from all walks of life. He was a humble, self-effacing man who learnt from all the experiences of his varied life. After all, he had been a soldier, a prisoner, a student, a lawyer, a judge, a husband, a father, an author, a persecuted nobody, a refugee, a theology student and, last but not least, the evangelistic minister of three parish churches.

He continued to preach in weakness until a few weeks before his death, still witnessing the blessing of God. Because of his ministry, there are many in heaven today. Though virtually blind, he wrote to the author encouraging the use of his writings, photographs and correspondence to convey this testimony to any who would listen to or read it.

If Werner Simonson could speak from the grave, he would doubtless be calling on all who have no relationship with God to be reconciled to their Creator by repentance and faith in the work of Jesus Christ on the cross, the benefits of which come directly to the individual soul by the sovereign grace of the Holy Spirit.

His little book of memories, *The Last Judgement*, sets out at the beginning his motive for writing: 'I have written this small book to show that God can change lives.' It is hard to argue with that in the face of Werner Simonson's experience.

More information on Werner Simonson

I corresponded with both Werner and his son Juergen.

Simonson's memoir, *The Last Judgement* (1969), was a small print run by publisher Colin Smythe of Gerrards Cross, England. It is no longer available in the UK, but has recently been translated into German.

When Werner died, the *Daily Telegraph* printed an accurate obituary, which sometimes adds to the details given in the book.

I would like to put on record my thanks to Juergen Simonson for the loan of photographs and his general support with this project.

13

Henry Gerecke

Chaplain to Nazi war criminals

> As Gerecke looked at the crimes of which the
> fifteen were accused he felt totally inadequate.
> 'How can a pastor, a Missouri farm boy,
> make any impression on these disciples of
> Adolf Hitler? How can I approach them? How
> can I summon the true Christian spirit that
> this mission demands of a chaplain?'

Henry Gerecke in the uniform of a US Army chaplain

13

Henry Gerecke

Visiting condemned men in their cells was nothing new to Henry Gerecke.

Much of his early career was devoted to work in prisons. However, the men he went to see in their cells at Nuremberg, Germany, just after midnight on Wednesday, 16 October 1946, were no ordinary prisoners. They were high-ranking Nazis sentenced to be hanged for the vilest crimes.

He walked with each of the ten condemned men from their cells to the gallows. He heard all their last words. Some expressed thanks and faith. Others stayed defiant to the end, their belief in Hitler still unshaken, even though he was dead. One condemned man even shouted, 'Heil Hitler!' on the gallows before taking the final drop into the darkness.

The story of Henry Gerecke is little known and the events of the most important year of his life, November 1945 to November 1946, have been largely overlooked. In that year he acted as spiritual adviser and chaplain to Nazis on trial before the International Military Tribunal at Nuremberg. His own accounts, written soon after the event while memory was fresh, survive in

American archives. From these primary sources the following story is compiled. He never asked to be believed. He simply outlined his experiences.

Henry F. Gerecke was born in August 1893, the child of a farmer and his wife living at Gordonville, Missouri, USA. The family was bilingual. Young Henry spoke as much German as English in his early years. The family was very active spiritually. At home he was taught to pray and trust the Bible as the Word of God. The family church was Lutheran, attached to the Missouri Synod. This is a decidedly evangelical body. Its beliefs were not unlike those of Reformer Martin Luther, with his emphasis on being right with God by personal faith in Christ, rather than by trying to achieve communion with God by accumulating good deeds, even religious good deeds.

After attending a local school during his early years, Henry spent 1913–1918 at St John's College, Winfield, Kansas. Then, in preparation for the ministry, he went to Concordia Seminary in St Louis. Ordained as a Lutheran pastor in 1926, he served as minister of Christ Lutheran Church, St Louis, until 1935. In that year he was appointed as executive director of St Louis Lutheran City Mission.

The chief task was coordinating aid to the underprivileged of St Louis. The mission was a large organization reaching institutions like hospitals, schools, nursing homes, refuges and jails. Gerecke led it from the front. An account of its work while Gerecke was in charge still exists. This reveals his extensive care and preaching ministry, notably in the city jail, which held murderers as well as other criminals.

Gerecke's own written rules for the mission's work emphasized the need for personal faith. He was interested in 'soul winning', an old expression for spreading the gospel of Christ. His basic advice to the mission's workers when confronted by the 'unchurched' was: 'Show them Jesus, Saviour from sin.'

Every Saturday for many years, Gerecke broadcast a programme on the local radio station KFUO called *Moments of Comfort*. Its main target was shut-ins, and those in hospital. A report from the time states, 'Many souls have been won for heaven.' It is plain from this evidence that Gerecke had clear-cut confidence that the message of the Bible would bring redemption, hope and comfort to those who responded in faith. 'Thousands of letters' received by the mission affirmed the point.

By 17 August 1943 the United States had been at war with Germany and Japan for nearly two years. On that day Henry Gerecke left St Louis to enter the Chaplains' School at Harvard. He was one of 253 Lutheran pastors from the Missouri Synod who became chaplains during World War II.

After a short time at Fort Jackson, Columbia, in South Carolina, he sailed for England in March 1944. The destination was the US Army's 98th General Hospital, where he served for fourteen months tending the sick and wounded. After D-Day, 6 June 1944, the trickle of casualties became a flood. In June 1945 he crossed to France with the hospital as it received the wounded brought back from the front lines.

A month later the hospital was in Munich. While in Germany he went to Dachau concentration camp, 'where my hand, touching a wall, was smeared with the human blood seeping through'. News had already been received that his eldest son Henry had been 'ripped apart', but not killed, in the fighting, and that his second son, Carlton, had been severely wounded in the Battle of the Bulge. His youngest son, Roy, had also entered the US Army. All in all he had had enough of war and was looking forward to going home. He had not seen his wife Alma for two and a half years, and working with the wounded and dying had been trying and unpleasant.

Then, early in November 1945, Gerecke was called into the office of his commanding officer, Colonel James Sullivan. The

fifty-two-year-old Gerecke had been assigned to the 6,850th
Internal Security Detachment at Nuremberg. Why? To serve
as spiritual adviser and chaplain to the top Nazi war criminals
on trial there. Sullivan offered his opinion that it was the most
unpopular assignment around. He told Gerecke that he did not
have to go. He encouraged him to use his age as a reason to return
to the inactive reserves in America. Gerecke wrote, 'I almost went
home.' He prayed for guidance. 'Slowly the men at Nuremberg
became to me just lost souls whom I was being asked to help.'[1]
After a few days he gave Colonel Sullivan his decision: 'I'll go.'

The US Army had selected Gerecke for three reasons: first, he
spoke German; secondly, he had extensive experience in prison
ministry and, lastly, he was a Lutheran Protestant. Fifteen of the
twenty-one Nazis on trial identified themselves as 'Protestant'.
Assisting him would be Roman Catholic chaplain Sixtus
O'Connor. Six of the prisoners claimed to be 'Roman Catholic'.

The most senior Nazis of all, such as Hitler, Himmler and
Goebbels, had already committed suicide to avoid justice. As
Gerecke looked at the crimes of which the fifteen were accused
he felt totally inadequate. 'How can a pastor, a Missouri farm boy,
make any impression on these disciples of Adolf Hitler? How can
I approach them? How can I summon the true Christian spirit
that this mission demands of a chaplain?' He prepared himself
by praying 'harder than I ever had in my life', so that he could
'somehow learn to hate the sin but love the sinner'.

The prison block at Nuremberg had three storeys. The Nazis
were on the ground floor. There was a broad corridor running its
length with cells on both sides. Each cell door had a window at
shoulder height. This let down to form a shelf where meals were
placed. The window was open at all times for observation. A guard
stood at the door of every cell round the clock and was required
to look at the prisoner once a minute. Only if there was a breach
of discipline was a guard allowed to speak to a prisoner. The

waiter who brought the food was not permitted to answer even a greeting. The rest of the building was used for the several hundred witnesses who would give evidence at this trial of the century.

Colonel Burton Andrus, the US commanding officer of the prison, made Gerecke's task clear. He would be allowed to conduct services for any Protestant Nazi prisoner who wanted to come, and be available for spiritual counsel, but only if invited by the prisoner. Nothing he said or did would influence the outcome of the trial. That was in other hands.

It was 12 November 1945—time to begin work. Gerecke decided that he would visit each prisoner. That experience provided him with his first impressions of the men on trial. He admitted later, 'I was terribly frightened.' There was nothing frightening in a physical sense, because the once all-powerful prisoners were now helpless. It was the nature of their crimes, their connection with the absolute depths of evil, which made Gerecke shudder.

Before going to the cells he made the decision to offer to shake hands with each of the accused. There was no intention of making light of what they had done. Gerecke wanted to be friendly so that his message would not be hindered by a wrong approach. In his 1947 account of his first visit to the cells, Gerecke records that he was criticized for this decision. Presumably his critics did not understand his spiritual motives.

The first cell contained fifty-one-year-old Rudolf Hess, who once had been Hitler's deputy in the Nazi party. Hess ruled his life by astrology. Gerecke offered his hand. Hess responded.

Speaking in German, Gerecke asked, 'Would you care to attend chapel service on Sunday evening?'

'No,' replied Hess, in English.

Gerecke then asked him, this time in English, 'Do you feel you can get along as well without attending as if you did?'

'I expect to be extremely busy preparing my defence,' answered

Hess. 'If I have any praying to do, I'll do it here.'[2]

Gerecke left, knowing that he had accomplished nothing.

The next cell contained the highest-ranking Nazi on trial, fifty-two year old former Luftwaffe chief Hermann Goering. With a range of powers given to him by Hitler, he had been an agent of death, clearly guilty of all charges. Gerecke wrote, 'I dreaded meeting the big flamboyant egotist worse than any of the others. Through the small aperture I had a chance to size him up for a moment. He was reading a book and smoking his meerschaum pipe.'[3]

Goering at the height of his power and pride

Any diffidence Gerecke felt was removed by Goering's shrewdly calcuated amiability. 'I am glad to see you,' said Goering,[4] pulling up a chair for Gerecke. In conversation, he seemed enthusiastic about attending chapel services, though the chaplain soon found out from the prison psychologist that he only went in order to get out of his cell for a while.

The third cell contained sixty-three-year-old Field Marshal Wilhelm Keitel, chief of the Supreme Command of the Armed Forces. His unquestioning obedience to Hitler led to his being responsible for more deaths than anybody could count. Gerecke found Keitel also reading a book. 'I asked him what he was

Extract from a scene at the Nuremberg trials showing, from left to right, in the front row, Goering, Hess, Ribbentrop and Keitel, and in the back row, Doenitz, Raeder, Schirach and Sauckel
(see page 267 for another view of the scene)

reading. He all but knocked me speechless by replying, "My Bible."'

Keitel then said, 'I know from this book that God can love a sinner like me.'

'A phoney,' thought Gerecke.

They talked. Yes, he would come to chapel. Would the chaplain join his devotions now? 'This I wanted to see,'[5] thought Gerecke.

Keitel knelt beside his bed and began to pray. He confessed his many sins and pleaded for mercy because of Christ's sacrifice for sin. When Keitel finished his prayer, both men repeated the Lord's Prayer together. Then Gerecke gave a benediction.

The next cell contained fifty-one-year-old Fritz Sauckel. Once Head of Labour Supply, he was, according to the Chief Justice Jackson, 'the greatest and cruellest slaver since the pharaohs of Egypt'.[6] He worked millions of slave labourers to death without mercy. When Gerecke appeared, he exclaimed with feeling: 'As a pastor, you are one person to whom I can open my heart.'[7] During the conversation that followed he wiped away many tears. Yes, he would attend chapel services.

Admiral Raeder agreed to attend. That was not surprising since it was he who had taken the initiative in asking for spiritual advice. 'Be sure to visit my friend Admiral Doenitz,' urged Raeder as Gerecke departed. In the event Doenitz, the man once in command of the U-boats, was not interested in spiritual matters. 'I'll attend your services,' was his lukewarm response to Gerecke.

He went to the next heavy door. Initial contact with fifty-two-year-old Joachim von Ribbentrop was not encouraging. He had been Hitler's foreign minister. He was best remembered in Britain for greeting King George VI with a 'Heil Hitler' salute while ambassador to the UK. He had a string of difficulties about Christian belief, which he shared with Gerecke in the months before the verdict. Nor would Ribbentrop promise to come to the service on Sunday, commenting that 'This business of religion isn't as serious as you consider it.'[8] In spite of this, he became a regular in the chapel.

Gerecke's footsteps echoed in the corridor as he proceeded to the cell of Alfred Rosenberg. The fifty-two-year-old Nazi 'philosopher' had committed most of his crimes while Minister for the Occupied Eastern Territories. He rejected everything Gerecke stood for, and told him to spend his time with others. Like Hess, he never attended any services.

Just a few paces further on and the chaplain found himself with Baron von Neurath. The latter had served Hitler as 'Reich protector' of Bohemia, in other words, ruler of most of occupied Czechoslovakia. To be invited to go to church was a new experience for the seventy-two-year-old aristocrat. Though very lukewarm on the subject of faith, he did ultimately attend services.

The next short walk took Gerecke to Hjalmar Schacht. He

was a sixty-eight-year-old banker who, as Nazi Economics Minister, had used his skills to finance pre-war German rearmament. He had little or no interest in spiritual matters, but informed Gerecke that if a Lutheran minister was holding services, he would be there.

Extract from a trial scene showing, from left to right, in the front row Rosenberg, Frank, Frick, Streicher, Funk and Schacht, and in the back row, Speer, von Neurath and Fritzsche

Next was fifty-five-year-old Walther Funk, head of the German Central Bank and head of the war economy. He was another banker who protested his innocence. The Allies took the view that a man who filled the bank's vaults with gold teeth and fillings taken from the mouths of the regime's victims was a war criminal. Funk decided to go to chapel.

A little further and Gerecke was with Hans Fritzsche. He was forty-five years old, and had been a senior figure in Goebbels' Ministry of Propaganda. He decided to attend merely to hear what the chaplain would say.

The chaplain's walk from cell to cell was nearly over. Next he met Baldur von Schirach. At the age of thirty-eight he was the youngest defendant, and had been the Hitler Youth leader.

Gerecke disliked the visit to Wilhelm Frick. He was sixty-eight and was a hard-line Nazi whose title, Minister of the Interior, covered up a vicious reign of terror.

The final man was forty-year-old Albert Speer, Minister of Armaments, who had caused as many deaths as any other man on trial. Every other Nazi claimed to be obeying orders. Speer probably saved himself from death by admitting responsibility and cooperating with his interrogators. He was to become known as 'the Nazi who said sorry'.

Frick, Speer and Schirach all said that they would come to chapel services.

As Sunday, 18 November 1945, approached, Gerecke wondered how many of these men, whose collective crimes were so immense, would in fact attend the service.

Knocking down the wall between two cells on the second floor made a spartan chapel. Where the organ came from is not explained, but the organist was a volunteer from among the witnesses. He was Walter Schellenberg, once a top officer in the Nazi security police. The simple services consisted of three hymns, a Scripture reading, prayers, a sermon and the benediction. Fifteen chairs were put out in hope. Out of a possible 'congregation' of fifteen, thirteen came—and continued to come on the following Sundays. Hess and Rosenberg kept their word and did not come.

For the first service only, two trial witnesses filled the two vacant seats. One was Hess's former secretary. The other was Field Marshal Kesselring. During the hymn singing Goering's voice always 'boomed above all the rest', and Gerecke noticed that Kesselring was moved to tears during the gospel sermon in German.

At the end of the service Sauckel asked to see Gerecke in his cell. When the chaplain arrived, he sensed that Sauckel wanted to discuss spiritual matters. After some conversation on those lines, Sauckel implored Gerecke to read the Bible and pray with him. Unafraid and unashamed, Sauckel prayed at his bedside and ended with the words: 'God be merciful to me a sinner.' In the weeks that followed Sauckel was given his own Bible and *Luther's Catechism*. Gerecke worked with Sauckel until he reached the point where he was satisfied in his own mind that the latter was a broken man with regard to what he had done. No restitution was possible, but Gerecke was convinced that Sauckel trusted in Christ as Saviour and had become a real Christian. In his written submissions about his work Gerecke repeatedly insisted: 'I have had many years of experience as a prison chaplain and I do not believe I am easily deluded by phoney reformations at the eleventh hour.'[9]

As Christmas 1945 approached, Gerecke noticed a change in the spiritual attitudes of Fritzsche, Schirach and Speer. After instruction in the Christian faith these three joined Sauckel and Schellenberg, the organist, as communicants. The Lutheran preparation to receive the bread and the wine ends with the pastor addressing each proposed communicant in these words: 'I now ask you before God, is this your sincere confession, that you heartily repent of your sins, believe on Jesus Christ, and sincerely and earnestly purpose, by the assistance of God the Holy Spirit, from now on to amend your sinful life? Then declare so by saying: "Yes."'[10]

The guards who were present at this first communion service were so impressed by the bearing of the penitent Nazis that they said to Gerecke, 'Chaplain, you'll not need us. This is holy business.'[11] They walked out, leaving Gerecke alone with his five communicants.

Gerecke wrote later, 'I am very slow about administering the Lord's Supper. I must feel convinced that each candidate not only understands its significance, but that, in penitence and faith, he is ready for the sacrament.'[12]

Keitel was to follow the road to faith. Gerecke recorded: 'On his knees and under deep emotional stress, he received the Body and Blood of our Saviour in the bread and the wine. With tears in his eyes he said, "May Christ, my Saviour, stand by me all the way. I shall need him so much."'[13]

In the spring of 1946 Raeder told Gerecke that he too wanted to be a Christian. He had stated initially that he could not accept certain Christian beliefs and Gerecke thought he was a genuine intellectual sceptic. He had a Bible and tried to dig for material to justify his doubts. After many services and much instruction in the meaning of Christian belief, he changed into 'a devout Bible student'. Eventually Gerecke added him to the communicants.

Even more heartening for the American pastor was 'the slow but steady change in von Ribbentrop'. In the course of several months he moved from cool, arrogant indifference to sincere questioning of Gerecke about various Christian teachings. He became more and more penitent, eager to turn from the past. After his final plea in the courtroom, Gerecke admitted him to communion, being convinced that God had worked in his soul.

Ribbentrop's wife agreed with her husband's pleadings that she should bring up their children in a godly way if the verdict went against him. Eventually, after instruction, Gerecke arranged for the Ribbentrop children to be baptized in the local church.

So it was that eight former Nazis were admitted to communion on the basis of their request, Gerecke's instruction and a believable profession of faith. That is the practice of almost all churches. There are no windows to look into men's souls. Gerecke acted in good faith on the basis of the evidence available in 1945–46. A biblical parallel for late repentance is the penitent thief on the cross at the side of Jesus who professed faith in the Lord as his end brought eternity into focus.

During the late spring of 1946 a rumour went round the war criminals that Gerecke, now nearing his fifty-third birthday, would be allowed to return home because of his age. Hans Fritzsche wrote a letter on 14 June 1946 addressed to Mrs Gerecke. This unusual document still exists in US archives. While the court was in session, and with permission, the letter went from one prisoner to another until all read it. Amazingly it was signed, not only by the Protestants, but also by the Roman Catholics—and by Hess and Rosenberg, the two who refused to attend chapel. It was sent through the regular prison censorship with a translation and a note of explanation sent by Gerecke to his wife. Gerecke's handwritten

18 June 46

My Dear!

Here's the most unusual letter signed on the original by the most talked about men in the World.

You are, without a doubt, the only woman in the world to get such a letter containing such a request. It is noteworthy that the Catholics too have signed it. Keep the letter for my book, Honey. Fritzsche wrote it and von Schirach translated it. Riffy May want it some day. Its not for the Press, but show it to your friends. Half of these men will go to their death. Oh yes, the signatures were gotten while they were sitting in Court, while von Papen was on the stand.

Love,

Hubby

Facsimile of letter sent by Henry Gerecke to his wife accompanying the letter signed by the Nazis letter, also still extant, says, 'Here's the most unusual letter signed on the original by the most talked about men in the world. You are, without a doubt, the only woman in the world to get such a letter containing such a request.' He goes on to say that of the twenty-one men who signed he expects that 'half will go to their death'.

The substance of the prisoners' letter says:

My dear Mrs Gerecke,

Your husband, Pastor Gerecke, has been taking religious care of the undersigned ... during the Nuremberg trial. He has been doing so for more than half a year.

We have now heard, dear Mrs Gerecke, that you wish to see him back home ... we understand this wish very well.

Nevertheless we are asking you to put off your wish to gather your family around you. Please consider that we cannot miss your husband now.

Our dear Chaplain Gerecke is necessary for us, not only as a pastor, but also as the thoroughly good man that he is.

In this stage of the trial it is impossible for any other man than him to break through the walls that have been built up around us, in a spiritual sense even stronger than in a material one. Therefore please leave him with us. We shall be deeply indebted to you.

We send our best wishes to you and your family. God be with you.[14]

Senior Nazis on trial at the International Military Tribunal, Nuremberg
(see also pages 265, 267)

Alma Gerecke sent an airmail reply: 'They need you.'

With reflection it seems a strange irony of history that men once so powerful should be reduced to petitioning an American housewife to allow her husband to continue to give them spiritual advice.

The trial ended on 31 August 1946. While the judges were in secret session Gerecke and O'Connor arranged for wives and children to visit provided that this took place before the verdicts were announced. Gerecke records several memories of the families. Goering's wife urged his child Edda to talk to Gerecke. Surprised, and thinking quickly of something to say, he asked the child if she said her prayers. The reply was: 'I pray every night.'

'And how do you pray?' persisted the chaplain.

She answered, 'I kneel by my bed and ask God to open my Daddy's heart and let Jesus in.'

When he tried to talk to Rosenberg's pretty thirteen-year-old, she interrupted: 'Don't give me any of that prayer stuff.' So Gerecke asked, 'Is there anything at all I can do for you?'

'Yes,' she answered. 'Got a cigarette?'[15]

On 1 October 1946 each of the defendants in turn stood alone in the dock for the verdict. Each man had been tried on four counts. In summary form they were:

1.Crimes against peace;

2. Planning a war;

3.War crimes;

4.Crimes against humanity.

Gerecke watched the members of his 'congregation' as each heard the verdict. Death sentences went to Goering, Ribbentrop, Keitel, Frick, Sauckel and Rosenberg; life imprisonment to Hess, Raeder and Funk; long terms of imprisonment to Schirach, Speer, von Neurath and Doenitz. Fritzsche and Schacht were declared not guilty. Five of the six Roman Catholics were sentenced to death.

Whatever else may be said about the Nuremberg Trials, it is impossible to deny that the defendants were given support and a hearing—something the guilty refused their own victims.

For reasons of security, chapel services ceased after the verdicts were given. Cell interviews numbered many hundreds up to this time. But before the executions on 16 October 1946, there were to be many more.

At about 20.30 on the evening before the death sentences were

Goering shortly before he committed suicide

carried out, Gerecke had his final talk with Goering, who was to hang first soon after midnight in the early hours of the morning of the 16th. During this final interview Goering denied the fundamentals of Christian belief—and then had the temerity to ask for the Lord's Supper. His attitude was: 'I'll take the Supper just in case there is anything to this business of yours.' What Gerecke told him supports the chaplain's own statement that he took the administration of the Lord's Supper seriously: 'I cannot give you the Lord's Supper because you deny the very Christ who instituted the sacrament ... you do not have faith in Christ and have not accepted him as your Saviour. Therefore you are not a Christian, and as a Christian pastor I cannot commune with you.'[16] Goering responded by saying, 'I'll take my chances.'[17]

At about 22.30 Goering committed suicide by swallowing potassium cyanide. Commander of the prison Colonel Andrus asked Gerecke to go round the cells and tell the others what Goering had done. They all took a dim view of the cowardice of a man who had bragged how brave he would be at the end. It was as if his lifelong pride had led to the almost inevitable nemesis.

That left ten men to die by the rope. At 01.00 Ribbentrop

was called for first. Before he walked to the gallows, he told Gerecke that he put all his trust in Christ. Ribbentrop was then marched to the first of three scaffolds. He climbed the thirteen steps to the trapdoor. The impassive soldiers and press representatives looked on. A guard tied his legs. An American officer asked for his last words. Ribbentrop responded: 'I place all my confidence in the Lamb who made atonement for my sins. May God have mercy on my soul.' Then

Another picture of Henry Gerecke.

he turned to Gerecke and said, 'I'll see *you* again.'[18] The black hood was pulled over his face. The thirteen-coiled noose was put round his neck—and he dropped through the trap door.

Keitel and Sauckel followed amidst similar scenes.

When it came to Frick's turn, Gerecke records that he received a surprise. Although Frick had been regular at chapel services, and unlike Rosenberg had accepted a Bible, he never showed faith. Andrus allowed Gerecke a few minutes in Frick's cell before he was escorted to the gallows. On the scaffold Frick, who never took communion, stood in front of the chaplain in his bright tweed jacket and told him that secretly during the chapel services he had come to believe that Christ had washed away his sins. Then the door opened beneath his feet and he was gone.

The last of Gerecke's group was Rosenberg. 'I asked if I might say a prayer with him. He smiled and said, "No, thank you." He lived without a Saviour, and that is the way he died.'[19]

Master Sergeant John C. Woods, the official executioner, had already hanged 347 men for various reasons. He was really looking forward to hanging the hated Nazis and filling the waiting coffins. By contrast, and for reasons he never explained, Gerecke was not totally convinced about death by hanging. To avoid future trouble the bodies of the eleven were cremated at Dachau a few hours later.

At 02.45, when the executions were over, Henry Gerecke walked from the scene to be alone. Later he wrote, 'Thus died eleven men of intelligence who, differently influenced, could have been, I am convinced, a blessing to the world instead of a curse.'[20]

Shortly afterwards Captain Gerecke was promoted to major. He left Nuremberg on 16 November 1946, and arrived back at St Louis, Missouri, in time to spend the first Christmas with his family for three years.

He was assigned as prison chaplain to the US Army Disciplinary Barracks at Milwaukee, Wisconsin. There he stayed for thirty-three months dealing with disobedient soldiers. He described them as 'mostly young men whom the world wanted to forget'.

His duties as 5th Army chaplain ended on 1 July 1950. He became a well-accepted joint pastor at St John Lutheran Church, Chester, Illinois. In parallel with this work he served as 'institutional missionary' to the 800 prisoners at the Menard State Penitentiary. Driving to take a Bible study at the prison, he collapsed at the gate on 11 October 1961. A heart attack killed him. He was only sixty-eight years old.

Warden Ross Randolph said of the deceased Gerecke, 'The prisoners respected him. He never lost his temper with them, and they knew they couldn't fool him.'[21]

The prisoners may have warmed to him, but after his death his eldest son, Henry, found a thick file of letters stored in a secret compartment in his father's desk. They were postmarked from all over the US. 'They called my father everything,' reported Henry Gerecke. 'He was called "Jew-hater", "Nazi-lover". They said that he should have been hanged at Nuremberg with the rest of them.' All the letters were written in the 'most hateful vituperative language imaginable'.[22]

The Christian concepts of grace and mercy have always been opposed, not only by the liberal intelligentsia and those with no spiritual interests, but also by a cross-section of most societies. The fact that Gerecke was called a 'Jew-hater' makes some historians suspicious that many of the letters came from unforgiving American Jews.

There were only three men among the Allies at Nuremberg who spoke German to the defendants—Dr Gilbert, the psychologist, O'Connor and Gerecke. They bore the burden of the spiritual response to the issue of guilt among the Nazis. Hans Fritzsche, who had been found not guilty, later wrote a book in which he offers his opinion: 'Of all the prison officials, the most outstanding was the insignificant-looking, unassuming, Lutheran pastor from St Louis, Gerecke.'[23]

More information on Henry Gerecke

The primary sources for this story are stored in the Concordia Historical Institute, St Louis, USA. This is the official archive for the history of Lutherans in America.

Pastor Victor Budgen wrote an article on the Nuremberg Trials in *Evangelical Times*, May 1985. He based his article on the book by F. T. Grossmith, *The Cross and the Swastika* (H. E. Walter. 1984). Paul Watkins of Stamford, England, published a second edition of this book in 1998. Sadly, Fred Grossmith died in April 2002. The book he wrote perpetuates the mistake that Albert Speer was truly converted. The evidence for the assertion that this was not the case is based on events in his later life, which were, in practice, a denial of the faith.

The only scholarly assessment of Gerecke's ministry at Nuremberg is by Dr Nicholas M. Railton of the University of Ulster. It is a long article called 'Henry Gerecke and the Saints of Nuremberg'. It appeared in English in a German magazine (*Kirchliche Zeitgeschichte*) in January 2000. Although Gerecke wrote on the subject several times, the primary document is *My Assignment with the International Military Tribunal at Nürnberg, Germany*, by Henry F. Gerecke, 13 May 1947. It makes astonishing reading.

The internet site of St John Lutheran Church, Chester, Illinois, USA, includes a talk given by him. Those who have the correct equipment can hear 'a voice from the past'.

Notes

Chapter 1—Louis Zamperini

1. Unless otherwise stated, quotations are taken with permission from: Louis Zamperini with David Rensin, *Devil at my Heels*. Copyright © 2003 by Louis Zamperini. Published by William Morrow, an imprint of HarperCollins Publishers, New York, USA, 2003.

Chapter 2—Paul Schneider

1. D. MacG. Jackson, *Moral Responsibility and Clinical Research*, Tyndale Press, 1958, p.17.
2. E. H. Robertson, *Paul Schneider: The Pastor of Buchenwald*, SCM Press, 1956, p.16.
3. *Ibid.*, p.21.
4. The story and quotations relating to the epileptic boy are in Robertson, *Paul Schneider: The Pastor of Buchenwald*, p.26.
5. The Barmen Declaration consists of six statements. The words cited here represent the essence of the first one. See Mary Bosanquet, *The Life and Death of Dietrich Bonhoeffer*, Hodder and Stoughton, 1968, p.142.
6. Claude R Foster, Jr., *Paul Schneider: The Buchenwald Apostle*, West Chester University Press, 1997, p.386.
7. *Ibid.*, p.386.
8. Victor Budgen, *Paul Schneider and the Nazis*, unpublished manuscript, no date, p.9.
9. Robertson, *Paul Schneider: The Pastor of Buchenwald*, p.56.
10. The conversation in which Gretel accuses Paul of not giving adequate consideration to his family is in Foster, *Paul Schneider: The Buchenwald Apostle*, p.684.
11. *Ibid.*, p.718.
12. Robertson, *Paul Schneider: The Pastor of Buchenwald*, p.93.
13. Foster, *Paul Schneider: The Buchenwald Apostle*, p.773.
14. *Ibid.*, p.806.
15. *Ibid.*, p.807.
16. *Ibid.*, p.817.
17. *Ibid.*, p.848.
18. *Ibid.*, p.848.

19. These are the words of an inmate, Alfred Leikam.

20. The reaction of Dietrich Bonhoeffer on hearing of Paul Schneider's murder is described in Foster, *Paul Schneider: The Buchenwald Apostle*, p.806.

21. Readers who want to know about the adult lives of the six children can contact the Pastor Paul Schneider Association.

Chapter 3—William Dobbie

1. S. Maxwell Coder, *Dobbie, Defender of Malta*, Moody Press, Chicago, USA, 1946, p.50.

2. *Ibid.*, p.51.

3. The words appear in an extract from the book published in *Practical Christianity* magazine (for officers of the three services), January-February 1965, p.2.

4. The beginning of his Christian life is almost always quoted in works about him. Probably the most complete account is in Sybil Dobbie, *Faith and Fortitude: The Life and Work of General Sir William Dobbie*, privately printed, 1979, pp.27–9.

5. Sybil Dobbie, *Faith and Fortitude*, p.114.

6. *Ibid.*, extracted from chapter 8, 'Letters from the War'.

7. *Ibid.*, p.120.

8. William Dobbie, *A Very Present Help*, Marshall, Morgan & Scott, Ltd, 1945, p.50.

9. *Ibid.*, p.51.

10. Ludendorff's remark is cited in many books about the First World War. I have referred to John Terraine, *The Great War*, Wordsworth edition, 1998, p.354.

11. William Dobbie, *A Very Present Help*, pp.52–3.

12. *Ibid.*, p.53.

13. Sybil Dobbie, *Faith and Fortitude*, p.177.

14. Major General A. J. H. Dove, 'Lieutenant General Sir William G. S. Dobbie, GCMG, KCB, DSO, LLD,' *Practical Christianity*, January-February 1965, p.19.

15. William Dobbie, *A Very Present Help*, p.83.

16. Sybil Dobbie, *Faith and Fortitude*, p.222.

17. *Ibid.*, p.222.

18. William Dobbie, *A Very Present Help*, p.89.

19. *Ibid.*, p.91.

20. Sybil Dobbie, *Faith and Fortitude*, p.306.

Chapter 4—Johanna-Ruth Dobschiner

1. All quotations are reproduced by permission of Hodder and Stoughton Ltd from *Selected to Live* by Johanna-Ruth Dobschiner.

Chapter 5—Charles Fraser-Smith

1. The opening dialogue is from a Bond film script quoted by Peter Worsley in 'Our English Heroes' (Charles Fraser-Smith) in *This England* magazine, Autumn 1998, p.18.
2. The telephone conversation is recorded in *The Secret War of Charles Fraser-Smith: The 'Q' Gadget Wizard of World War II*, Michael Joseph Ltd., 1981, p.25.
3. Quoted from personal correspondence.
4. Richard Wilkins, 'The Member who was "Q" ', Obituary in *ACT NOW* magazine, Spring 1993 issue, p.53.
5. Worsley, 'Our English Heroes', p.18.
6. Charles Fraser-Smith, *Secret Warriors*, Paternoster Press, 1984, p.58.
7. Peter Worsley, quoted in Crusader *LINK* magazine, obituary of Fraser-Smith, May 1993 issue, p.17. Charles Fraser-Smith was an active associate of this movement until his death, although he did not approve of some of the recent changes in it. He had attended a Crusader Bible class as a youngster, and in addition to his other duties, he had taught in the Rickmansworth class every Sunday afternoon throughout the war years.

Chapter 6—Mitsuo Fuchida

1. To aid identification, most Japanese aircraft were given easy-to-remember names.
2. Mitsuo Fuchida, *From Pearl Harbor to Calvary*, Bible Literature International, no date, p.5.
3. Gordon W. Prange with Donald M. Goldstein and Katherine V. Dillon, *God's Samurai*, Brassey's (US) Inc., 1990, p.3.
4. Fuchida, *From Pearl Harbor to Calvary*, p.8.
5. Elizabeth Sherrill, 'I'll never forget you—Mitsuo Fuchida,' *Guideposts* magazine, December 1991, p.43.
6. Prange, Goldstein & Dillon, *God's Samurai*, p.243.
7. Fuchida, *From Pearl Harbor to Calvary*, p.9.

8. Eugene Horle, 'I'll Always Remember Pearl Harbor,' *Power for Living* (take-home paper), Scripture Press, Inc., 4 December 1966.

9. Prange, Goldstein & Dillon, *God's Samurai*, p.260.

Chapter 7—Jacob DeShazer

1. C. Hoyt Watson, *The Amazing Story of Sergeant Jacob DeShazer*, Light and Life Press, Indiana, USA, 1950, p.28.

2. David Seamonds, 'The Kamikaze of God', *Christianity Today*, 3 December 2001.

3. Watson, *The Amazing Story of Sergeant Jacob DeShazer*, p.31.

4. Carroll V. Glines, *The Doolittle Raid*, Jove edition 1998, p.67.

5. Jacob DeShazer, *I was a Prisoner of Japan*, Bible Meditation League, 1950, p.1. This is the leaflet the front cover of which is illustrated on page 148.

6. Craig Nelson, *The First Heroes*, Corgi, 2002, p.416.

7. Quotations and information from Watson, *The Amazing Story of Sergeant Jacob DeShazer*, pp.97–8.

8. *Ibid.*, pp.99–100.

9. *Ibid.*, p.102.

10. *Ibid.*, p.117.

11. *Ibid.*, pp.121–2.

Chapter 8—Ernest Gordon

1. Unless otherwise stated, all the quotations are taken from *To End All Wars* by Ernest Gordon. Copyright © 2002 by Alastair Gordon. Used by permission of the Zondervan Corporation. Those who wish to read Ernest Gordon's book should ask for *To End All Wars*. (The title *Miracle on the River Kwai* is now only available second-hand.)

Chapter 9—Rupert Lonsdale

1. C. E. T. Warren and James Benson, *Will Not We Fear*, White Lion Publishers, 1973, p.107.

2. Rev. R. P. Lonsdale, *Who Does Care?* (Published privately, February 1987), p.1. All the other quotations derive from personal correspondence.

Chapter 10—Donald Caskie

1. *Life and Work* magazine, obituary notice, February 1984, p.44. Unless otherwise stated, all the other quotations are taken from: Donald Caskie, *The Tartan Pimpernel*, Fontana, 1960. Birlinn Ltd published a new edition in 1999.

Chapter 11—Michiharu Shinya

1. The quotations in the final two paragraphs of the story are the words of Mr Shinya taken from correspondence with the author. All the other quotations are taken with permission from Michiharu Shinya, *Beyond Death and Dishonour*, Castle Publishing Ltd., P.O. Box 68—100 Newton, Auckland, New Zealand, 2001. Castle's list of titles can be procured from this email address: info@castlepublishing.co.nz.

Chapter 12—Werner Simonson

1. All the quotations are taken with permission from Werner Simonson, *The Last Judgement*, Colin Smythe Ltd., Gerrards Cross, England, 1979.

Chapter 13—Henry Gerecke

Gerecke spoke and wrote of his experiences several times, both in Lutheran journals and in secular publications. The essential facts are identical, whether spoken or written, no matter which source is used. His stated motive, given in his talk preserved by St John's Church, is to save the story from being forgotten when Chaplain O'Connor and himself were 'six feet under'.

1. Gerecke's account of the conversation with Sullivan may be heard in his own words by downloading the talk from the website of St. John Lutheran Church, Chester, Illinois, USA (www.stjohnchester.com/).
2. All the quotations relating to Hess are from Henry Gerecke, 'I Walked to the Gallows with the Nazi Chiefs,' *Saturday Evening Post*, 1 September 1951, pp.18–19. The bimonthly *Saturday Evening Post* is still published in Indianapolis, USA.
3. *Ibid.*, p.19.
4. *Ibid.*
5. Conversation with Keitel, *ibid.*

6. F. T. Grossmith, *The Cross and the Swastika*, Henry E. Walter Ltd., Worthing, England, 1984, p.37.
7. *Saturday Evening Post*, p.19.
8. *Ibid.*, p.57.
9. *Ibid.*, p.18.
10. Grossmith, *The Cross and the Swastika*, p.68.
11. Henry Gerecke, talk on the St John's website.
12. *Saturday Evening Post*, p.18.
13. *Ibid.*, p.57.
14. Extracted from N. M. Railton, *Henry Gerecke and the Saints of Nuremberg*, Kirkliche Zeitgeschichte, Vandenhoeck and Ruprecht, 2000, pp.126–7.
15. The conversations with the children of Goering and Rosenberg are recorded in *Saturday Evening Post*, p.58. They are also a feature of Gerecke's talk on the St John's website.
16. *Ibid.*, p.58.
17. *Ibid.*
18. Henry Gerecke, 'Walther League Messenger', *Nuernberg Chaplain*, October 1947, p.15.
19. *Ibid.*
20. *Saturday Evening Post*, p.58.
21. Report in local newspaper.
22. David Strand, *The Lutheran Witness*, May 1995, p.23. In 2002 an article appeared on the Internet repeating the same information from a different angle and adding to it. See Keith Lockwood, 'Wartime Angst', in a feature called *Skeletons in our Closet* (http://jemimef.topcities.com).
23. Hans Fritzsche, *The Sword in the Scales*, London, 1953, p.55.

Note regarding copyright

In spite of serious endeavours to secure the permissions required, I am conscious that it is possible that some may have eluded me. If an error has been made, it will have been inadvertent. Apologies are offered with genuine sincerity. Such copyright holders are invited to contact the publisher so that matters may be rectified.

Picture credits

Chapter 1—Louis Zamperini

Louis Zamperini in 1945; Louis Zamperini in training at the Olympic Village, Berlin 1936—*Louis Zamperini*

A B-24 Liberator bomber—*Phil Butler*

Chapter 2—Paul Schneider

Paul Schneider while assistant pastor at Essen; Paul Schneider and Margarete Dieterich; Gretel Schneider with her six children—*Helen Harrop/The Pastor Paul Schneider Association*

Map of places associated with the life of Paul Schneider—*Claude Foster Jr*

Photograph of Paul Schneider in the cell at Buchenwald—*Friedrich Langer*

Chapter 3—William Dobbie

Lt-Gen. Sir William Dobbie—*J. Russell and Sons*

Chapter 4—Johanna-Ruth Dobschner

Johanna-Ruth Dobschiner—*Johanna-Ruth Dobschiner*

Chapter 5—Charles Fraser-Smith

Charles Fraser-Smith—*Mrs Lin Fraser-Smith*

Charles Fraser-Smith's official pass, 1942; A fountain pen with a hollow compartment to hold a compass; A shaving brush with a secret compartment in the handle; Dominoes sent to prisoners of war and SOE agents; A miniature radio—*Brian Fraser-Smith*

A box of 'Q' pencils; A 'Q' pencil broken to reveal a map—*David Tee*

Chapter 6—Mitsuo Fuchida

Mitsuo Fuchida—*Lane Anderson/Ken Anderson films*

A Japanese Nakajima B5N ('Kate')—*Phil Butler*

Front page of a tract written by Fuchida—*The Pocket Testament League (now known as 'Bridge-Builders')*

Chapter 7—Jacob DeShazer

Jacob DeShazer—*Carol Dixon*
A B-25 Mitchell bomber—*Phil Butler*
Front page of a tract by Jacob DeShazer—*Jim Falkenberg (Cook Communications Ministries)*
Jacob DeShazer in later life—*Jacob DeShazer*

Chapter 8—Ernest Gordon

Ernest Gordon while president of CREED—*Ernest Gordon*
The cemetery at Chungkai—*Commonwealth War Graves Commission*
Ernest Gordon in Singapore in 1942—*Gillian and Alastair Gordon*

Chapter 9—Rupert Lonsdale

Rupert Lonsdale; Rupert Lonsdale in full-dress naval uniform—*Rupert Lonsdale*
An Arado 196 German seaplane—*Phil Butler*
Sketches drawn by Signalman Waddington to show Seal's predicament and the final attempt to raise Seal—*Signalman Waddington*
Artist's impression of the deliverance of Seal—*Peter N. Millward*

Chapter 10—Donald Caskie

Donald Caskie in chaplain's uniform—*The National Library of Scotland*
Donald Caskie receives his 'big red book' from Eamonn Andrews—*Gordon Caskie*

Chapter 11—Michiharu Shinya

Michiharu Shinya when principal of Japan Biblical Seminary; Sub-lieutenant Michiharu Shinya in 1942—*Michiharu Shinya*
Akatsuki—*Tamiya Kits*
Map of places mentioned in the story of Michiharu Shinya; The group that met for Bible study; The prisoners leave Featherston camp; Mr and Mrs Shinya in Yokohama—*Castle Publishing*

Pastor Hessell Troughton—Doreen Payne

Chapter 12—Werner Simonson

Werner Simonson—*Werner Simonson* (© *Harrow Observer*)

Werner Simonson while a prisoner of war in France; Werner and Leonie
  Simonson on their wedding day; Front page of Werner Simonson's passport—
  Juergen Simonson

 Cuttings from newspapers reporting Werner Simonson's ordination—*Werner
  Simonson* (© *Fulham Chronicle, Illustrated London News, Evening Star*)

Chapter 13—Henry Gerecke

Henry Gerecke in the uniform of a US Army chaplain; Letter sent by Henry
  Gerecke to his wife; Henry Gerecke—*Concordia Historical Institute*

Goering at the height of his power—*David & Charles (publishers)*

Extracts from a scene at the Nuremberg trials—*Florida Center for Instructional
  Technology*

Senior Nazis on trial at Nuremberg; Goering shortly before he committed
  suicide—*Jewish Virtual Library*